BEST of BREED

LHASA APSO

JULIETTE CUNLIFFE

ACKNOWLEDGEMENTS

The publishers would like to thank the following for help with photography: Helen Bell; Wendy Cain (Kutani); Juliette Cunliffe; Carol Ann Johnson; Rob and Doreen Richardson (Belazieth); Hearing Dogs for Deaf People; Pets As Therapy.

Cover photo: © Tracy Morgan Animal Photography (www.animalphotographer.co.uk)
Dog featured is Nedlik A Splashing Moment (Lynden), owned by Sue Ellis.

Pages 15, 56 and 143 © istockphoto.com/Ruth Black; page 25 © istockphoto.com/Jonathan Barton
page 49 © istockphoto.com/Daydreams Girl; page 57 © istockphoto.com/Dorota Stawicka

The British Breed Standard reproduced in Chapter 7 is the copyright of the Kennel Club and published with the club's kind permission. Extracts from the American Breed Standard are reproduced by kind permission of the American Kennel Club.

THE QUESTION OF GENDER

The 'he' pronoun is used throughout this book instead of the rather impersonal 'it',
but no gender bias is intended.

First published in 2010 by The Pet Book Publishing Company Limited
PO Box 8, Lydney, Gloucestershire GL15 6YD

ISBN
978-1-906305-27-7
1-906305-27-7

Printed and bound in Singapore

CONTENTS

GETTING TO KNOW LHASA APSOS

A breed that hails from Tibet's high tablelands, the Lhasa Apso is very different from other breeds of dog, for it has a typically 'Tibetan' temperament. Apsos can be absolutely wonderful companions and are usually devoted to their owners, but it is they who decide which people are to be their friends, not the other way around.

The Apso is small in size, so is manageable, but the coat is undoubtedly high maintenance. Even if a pet Lhasa Apso is kept in what is called 'puppy trim', this still requires regular attention. The term 'Apso' or 'Apsok' is actually used by the Tibetans for any long-coated breed of dog, but when the complete name 'Lhasa Apso' is abbreviated, the term 'Apso' is the one that should be used, not 'Lhasa', which has sadly crept

into modern parlance today. When speaking of this breed the Tibetans use 'Apso', or sometimes 'Lhasa Apso', for they know that it is the name we use in the West, but of course the breed does not just hail from Tibet's capital, Lhasa, but from all over Tibet.

A TYPICAL LHASA APSO

This attractive small breed is often described as a 'big dog in a small body', for he is full of character and has an assertive manner. In his Tibetan homeland he was kept in monasteries to give a warning bark to the monks when visitors or intruders managed to get past the large, ferocious Tibetan Mastiffs that were tethered outside. The Apso was also kept in people's homes, especially by the more wealthy, and was used to protect their goods and chattels. This brief insight into the Apso's history is

indicative of his alertness and intelligence, and also his voice. However, he will usually accept his owner's command to be quiet, but not until he is sure the visitor has been accepted.

According to the English Kennel Club's Breed Standard, which effectively paints a verbal picture of the breed, the Lhasa Apso stands 25 cms (10 ins) at the shoulder; bitches should be slightly smaller. Sizes, though, vary quite considerably, in part because the American Breed Standard requires a slightly larger dog, so this has had an influence on some lines of breeding in the UK, too. However, the size as indicated by the English Kennel Club is what all breeders here should be aiming for. No weight is specified for this breed, but this is a sturdy dog and typically ranges between 6.3 and 8.4 kg (14-18.5 lbs). In outline, the Lhasa Apso is longer than it is

The size of a Lhasa Apso may vary, but it should be longer than it is high.

high, but it is by no means excessively long.

The Lhasa Apso's glorious coat is something that sets the breed apart from most other dogs. Not only is it long and luxuriant, but its texture is hard, something that has developed over generations to cope with the climate in Tibet. There is also an undercoat, which is now described in the Breed Standard as 'moderate', though it used to read 'dense'. This is highly important, as it provides protection against the elements and its insulating qualities keep the dog warm, even in the coldest climes. In the space of a

day, temperatures can easily vary from below zero to 38 degrees centigrade, and in the north and west of Tibet, temperatures can drop to minus 40 degrees.

Another highly characteristic feature of the breed is the headfall over the eyes. The Breed Standard in Britain has recently been changed slightly (see Chapter Seven: The Perfect Lhasa Apso), but until January of 2009 it used to require heavy head furnishings with a good fall over the eyes. In my personal estimation, this is absolutely essential. In Tibet where, after all, this breed was created, the light

is enormously bright and the snow incredibly white, so damage to the eyes must be avoided at all costs. Something that has never been mentioned in the Breed Standards is that the Apso has very long eyelashes, which serve the purpose of keeping the fall of hair out of the eyes, and so preventing damage. In consequence, the fall over the eyes forms a veil, which acts like sunglasses.

Think of the Tibetans who escaped from their troubled homeland over the mountainous passes into Nepal. They had no actual sunglasses, but those who

A DOG FOR ALLERGY SUFFERERS

It is important to owners of the breed to understand that the Apso's coat does not shed. Much of the undercoat is combed out when grooming, but if this is not done, the coat will mat, right down to the skin. Therefore, coat care is an essential part of good maintenance if a Lhasa Apso is to join your household. But because the coat does not shed, neither does it distribute hairs all around the home, and this is usually a fairly suitable breed for people who suffer from an allergy to canine hair.

realised what damage the bright, white light could do to their eyes cut tiny strips in pieces of cardboard, or even fabric, enabling them still to see, while offering protection from the glare. Indeed, I have met many Tibetan refugees who have travelled the passes without such protection and they suffered snow blindness and often long-term damage to their eyesight. So let us never forget that the Lhasa Apso really does need a good fall of hair over the eyes.

The Lhasa Apso is what is known as a partial-brachycephalic breed. Its foreface is reasonably short, but not as short as that of the Pekingese or Shih Tzu, with which the breed is closely related. The length of muzzle from the tip of the nose to the stop (the indentation between the eyes) is about 4 cms (1.5 ins). This is about one third of the total length from nose-tip to occiput (the bony protuberance at the back of the skull). The eye is dark, oval and of medium size,

The headfall serves a very useful purpose, providing protection from the bright, white light that dogs would have experienced in their native home, and still do.

APSO COLOURS

Pale cream.

Gold.

Black.

Particolour.

The stark landscape of Tibet, native home of the Lhasa Apso.
© *Juliette Cunliffe*

and its shape has been described as being like that of a human, which I have always felt sums it up nicely. Eyes that are too round and too full are an indication that the skull shape and eye socket are untypical of the breed.

GALAXY OF COLOURS

The Apso comes in almost every natural colour you can think of, as virtually all coat colours are acceptable. They can range from a pale cream, through various shades of gold and grey, to a deep black. In a true black the skin is blue, whereas in others the coat can look black during a dog's early years and then will most probably turn to grey. There are silver sables and gold sables and particolours too, just one of the reasons why seeing a class full of well-groomed show Apsos in the judging ring is a veritable joy.

Although no colours are unacceptable, the fact that the Breed Standard requires the nose to be black prevents liver and chocolate Apsos being shown, for these coat colours have corresponding pigment. These colours are produced from time to time, and in Tibet they are as well accepted as the other colours.

Later you will be have a chance to read the Breed Standards as published for different countries, but generally the Lhasa Apso should have a tight reverse scissor bite, so that the lower incisor teeth protrude very slightly beyond the upper ones. This is highly characteristic, but it is a difficult mouth to breed and you often find Apsos that are too undershot or that have a normal scissor bite, as most breeds of dog do. Sometimes the incisors meet exactly edge to edge, which is known as a level bite, and this is acceptable in the US. It is of interest to note that a level bite was included in Britain's first Standard for the breed, published in 1934, as was a slightly undershot one.

Because of the relative shortness of the muzzle, the teeth are packed fairly tightly into the mouth, though the incisors should be in as broad and straight a line as possible. However, this means that tooth care is essential, and, even from an early age, owners should get their dogs used to having their teeth cleaned regularly to prevent the occurrence of dental problems and gum disease.

STRUCTURE AND MOVEMENT

To understand the breed's construction, it is again necessary to visualise the geographical terrain in which the Apso's ancestors lived. Tibet is known as The Roof of the World; it is a mystical country with a barren landscape, situated at a high altitude. Because Tibet is in the Himalayan rain shadow, it is dry and sunny throughout the year, with heavy snowfalls less common than we might imagine.

The Lhasa Apso must be built correctly to move freely and effortlessly.

Flooding, though, can be a serious problem, for the sun is quick to melt the snows. Although there are many notably high mountains, the greatest of them all being Everest (known by the Tibetans as Chomolungma), the plains around Lhasa are about 10,000 feet (3,000 metres) above sea level, though when travelling overland, much higher passes have to be crossed.

If a dog is to survive successfully at this altitude, there must be adequate heart and lung space, so the ribs need to be capacious and extended well back, leading to a strong loin, which is not too long, for the Lhasa Apso is 'balanced and

WHEN IS AN APSO NOT AN APSO?

Occasionally, two full-coated parents can produce one or more puppies in a litter that more closely resemble a Tibetan Spaniel in appearance, the coat being much shorter. These pups are called 'Prapsos', or sometimes 'Perhapsos'. They appear in all colours, although the coat texture seems to vary sometimes according to coat colour. Generally the forelegs and feet are smooth, but there is some feathering between the toes and between the elbow and ankle. There is also feathering on the hindquarters, and the tail is well plumed. However, there is a lack of head furnishing and the body coat is either short and smooth or fairly short. The feet are rather finer and narrower than the cat-like foot of a typical Lhasa Apso.

Other puppies in the litter can develop perfectly normally.

In the 1960s, the late Thelma Morgan , a dedicated and knowledgeable early breeder whose stock often, but not always, carried the Ffrith affix, worked out some ratios and discovered that as many as six per cent of Lhasa Apsos were born as Prapsos. Indeed they are still produced, hopefully fewer in recent years, but unfortunately owners tend not to talk about them. However, puppy buyers should be aware that they might just come across a Prapso in a litter, so should be on the alert for these signs when picking a puppy. No Prapso should be bred from and, of course, a Prapso is not a suitable candidate for the show ring!

compact'. When standing the topline should be level and this should be retained on the move, the gait being free and jaunty.

The Lhasa Apso is a very stylish breed, but should never be over-exaggerated in any way. When observing an Apso as it moves away, you should never be able to see the full pad, as is the case for the Shih Tzu. In a Lhasa Apso, it should only be possible to see one third of the pad. Shoulders should be well laid back, allowing the dog to move freely; it is when an Apso is too upright in the shoulder that the full pads are shown, for the forelegs cannot extend out sufficiently well in front to balance with the rear movement. Forelegs should be straight and certainly not bowed as, sadly, is often found in the breed. Having said that, there is usually a slight curvature to the inner edge of the foreleg in order to accommodate the ribbing, but the outside should ideally be straight.

The Apso's lovely, high-set tail puts the finishing touch to the picture. It is carried well over the back and its long hair blends beautifully into the body coat, reaching to the ground in a fully coated adult.

THE APSO AS A COMPANION DOG
The Lhasa Apso is a companion dog, and a wonderful friend he can be, whether kept as a pet or a show dog. He has a very special character and each seems to have his or her own individual

As a companion dog, the Apso is second to none.   © *Carol Ann Johnson*

personality, but even a single dog's personality seems to change as the mood takes him.

He can be very aloof, and although he will probably be happy to join in with most things around the house, he expects his owner to allow him to decide exactly to what extent he wishes to be involved. One day he may seem to thoroughly enjoy doing the household chores and perhaps helping with a bit of gardening, while on another

occasion he may prefer just to sit and watch from a distance. If he decides not to take part in whatever activity is on offer, don't force him to join in. He will already have taken a firm decision and considers this his prerogative.

PET OR SHOW
Hopefully if you decide the Lhasa Apso is the right choice of dog for you and your family, you will have done so for many good

Do you have ambitions to show your Lhasa Apso?

ring. However, I do tend to clip them down when they reach well into double figures, as they can cope less easily with the laborious task of bathing, grooming and drying a long coat. There are many owners of show dogs who clip off their Lhasa Apsos immediately after retiring them from the ring, and this is quite understandable too, just so long as the coat, be it long or short, is kept in tip-top condition.

If a Lhasa Apso is kept purely as a pet, most owners clip down the coat, or, more likely, have it clipped by a professional dog groomer three or four times a year. This, of course, costs a fair amount of money each time, but it is nowhere near the expense of purchasing the many grooming products that are necessary to retain an Apso's glorious show coat. When Apsos are clipped down they can join in every type of activity their owners wish, without worrying too much about an enormous amount of work afterwards in sorting out the coat.

Long-coated Apsos can also join in the fun, especially if their coats are of the correct hard quality. I recall taking a Champion bitch of my own to Weston-super-Mare on the way back from a show. The sea was out but I was determined to reach it, though I hadn't realised quite how far out it was. My friend and I plodded on and on through the sand with her, having a wonderful time, but never reaching the tantalising blue waves. Before getting back into

reasons, not just the breed's glamour. There is no doubting that a Lhasa Apso is considered a 'glamour breed' but it is much, much more than that. The Apso temperament is different from most other dogs and will need a special kind of person to understand it. Those who truly love Lhasa Apsos love them for life, not just for the dog's life, but for the duration of their own, too. Those who like the breed only for its glamour are owners who fall

into a different category and will probably go out of the breed when the novelty has waned or when they discover it was not so easy to win in the show ring as they had originally thought.

It is perfectly possible to combine the best of both worlds and to have a dog as a show dog and as a pet. I am one of many such owners who fall into this category, and I keep my Apsos in full coat even after they have finished their career in the show

In most cases, an Aspo will get on better living with a family that has older children.

the car, we rinsed off the coat under a water tap on the sea front before putting our Apso back in the car, wrapped up in towels until we reached home. When we got back, she went straight into the bath and had a particularly thorough wash and groom – twice over, in fact! Yes, show dogs can enjoy romps too, but their owners have to be prepared to work rather harder at the coat!

APSOS AND CHILDREN

Many Apsos get along well with children, but others prefer to give them a wide berth. A lot depends on whether or not the Apso has been bred in a house that includes children, in which case they will have been exposed to them from an early age. Personally, I never sell Apsos to people who have children under the age of about seven years, for

until then children can be all too anxious to tug at an Apso's long, flowing locks. This can be painful for any long-coated breed, and an Apso will not always tolerate such attentions, however well intended.

Children can also be noisy, and I find that not all Apsos appreciate this, perhaps believing they were destined for a quieter monastic or more

The Lhasa Apso does not think of himself as being small, so he has no problem getting on with large dogs, such as this Deerhound.
© *Carol Ann Johnson*

stately life! I am certain there are some Apsos out there who enjoy the hub-bub of active family life, but I feel certain there are many more who prefer to live a more settled existence, perhaps with just one person, a couple, or a small, quietly mannered family.

APSOS AND OTHER PETS

Undoubtedly, Lhasa Apsos' temperaments vary quite considerably, some being very much more laid back then others. Although this breed is absolutely not a terrier, it does have a bit of a terrier temperament in some regards. I have one particular bitch who dearly loves to curl up in the same bed as one of my Whippets, but when the Whippet runs up or down the stairs, this same Apso will rush after her and snap at her heels for she is always ready to chase and to catch if she can. On the other hand, her son is as laid back as they come. I cite this as an example, purely to show you how very different they can be, even when closely related.

Apsos generally get along well with other dogs, but, like many small dogs, they seem to have no idea about their diminutive stature and therefore have no fear of larger animals. I have always kept Lhasa Apsos with sighthounds – Afghan Hounds, Whippets and Deerhounds –

Adults can be very playful and will get all the exercise they need romping in the garden.

and in most cases they have got along perfectly well, though sensible introductions and subsequent control is always important.

From personal experience, I have found that male Apsos do not always get along well together, especially when they have been used at stud, and yet my own male Apsos have always enjoyed the company of males of other breeds. Bitches generally get along well with each other, but there can be disagreements, which need strict control, especially around the time of a bitch's season.

Lhasa Apsos usually get along well with other pets, but some would be only too happy to chase a mouse or hamster if the opportunity arose. As with all things, so much depends upon training during a dog's early life and the introduction to other household pets. Apsos and cats usually get along well together, or at least show each other due respect!

EXERCISE
The Lhasa Apso does not need a great deal of exercise, but nonetheless he will always appreciate a good walk so that he can investigate new sights and smells to stimulate his senses. However, if your Apso is kept in long coat, you will have to pay special attention to where he is exercised, as his flowing robes

will pick up every ounce of dirt and debris, so will need to be carefully tended to upon returning home. Obviously, he will need an exercise area at home, so a garden, not necessarily a large one, is important to him.

If two Apsos are kept together and get along well because they have been carefully introduced to each other and have developed a friendship, they will spend many a happy hour exercising each other. They will love to romp and play together, and, in doing so, will use up considerably more energy than they would if they lived alone.

Apsos kept in short coat can be given considerably more freedom with regard to where they are exercised, but even a short coat can get wet and dirty, so will need checking over at the end of each walk.

HEALTH ISSUES

Like all breeds of dog, and mongrels and crossbreeds too, there are certain health issues connected with the breed, but to be forewarned is to be forearmed. The only health check that is currently required prior to mating in the UK is that for progressive retinal atrophy (PRA), a

THE LONG-LIVED LHASA APSO

The Lhasa Apso is well known for being a long-lived breed. Most of mine have lived to 14, 15 , and even 16 years, and there are several occasions when Apsos have lived longer than this. So, bearing this in mind, when you take on a Lhasa Apso puppy, you must be prepared to be his true companion for many a long year ahead.

congenital eye disease; both sire and dam must be tested before a mating takes place. More information relating to the health of the Lhasa Apso will be found in Chapter 8.

ASSISTANCE DOGS

THERAPY DOGS
Some Lhasa Apsos can make wonderful therapy dogs. When they are well trained and taken along to homes to visit the elderly or infirm, they are very popular visitors. Their small size and yet sturdy build makes them ideal for sitting on people's laps should they be allowed to do so. It is great to know that your Apso is giving pleasure to someone else who needs canine companionship but is unable to have this on a permanent basis.

However, I must stress that not all Apsos are suitable for this work. Granted, it takes very special training, but the personality of many Lhasa Apsos would simply not be suitable, due to their varied temperaments. We should always keep in mind that, in earlier Breed Standards, this breed was said to be "chary of strangers" and this is still true of many typical specimens of the breed today. In the 1980s the wording was changed to "somewhat aloof with strangers" and if an Apso is truly typical, it is not the sort of dog that accepts everyone. A typical Apso will choose who it wishes to approach and when, and this may not therefore be a temperament that is conducive to therapy work.

HEARING DOGS
The Lhasa Apso's alert hearing makes him a good contender as a Hearing Dog for Deaf People. He can be trained to alert his owner to sounds like that of the doorbell or telephone ringing, the alarm clock or even things like fire alarms. A well-trained Hearing Dog can make all the difference in the world to someone with impaired hearing.

HEARING DOGS

Hearing Dog Yogi.

Hearing Dog Rumour.

THE FIRST LHASA APSOS

Chapter 2

Tibet is a land of mystery, and there is also a certain mystery about the remarkable breeds of dog who live there. There have been claims that the Lhasa Apso has been in existence since 800 BC but, although this may be true, it cannot be substantiated for Tibet's earliest written records date back only to AD 639. It was during the seventh century that Buddhism spread into Tibet from India and it was in Buddhism that the lion, in its various mythological forms, played an important role.

The Lhasa Apso has often been likened to a lion dog and Buddha Manjusri, the god of learning, is believed to travel around as a simple priest, with a small dog that can be transformed into a lion so that the Buddha can ride on its back. But the lion with which the Lhasa Apso is most closely associated is the Snow Lion, a mythological beast that is believed to be so powerful that, when it roars, seven dragons fall out of the sky.

It is likely that the Lhasa Apso originally descended from European and Asiatic herding dogs, such as the Puli and Pumi, as indeed did the breed's close

The chosen dogs of nobility and monks, Apsos have even lived in the Potola Palace, former home of His Holiness The Dalai Lama. © *Juliette Cunliffe*

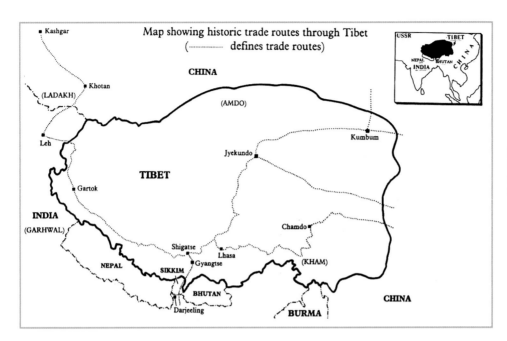

Map showing historic trade routes through Tibet
(·········· defines trade routes)

The journey from Tibet to China was notoriously difficult and dangerous.

The breed was – and still is – held in high esteem in its native home.
© *Juliette Cunliffe*

cousin, the Tibetan Terrier. We learned in the previous chapter that the Apso was kept not only in monasteries, but was also owned by wealthier families, such as nobles and merchants, the latter sometimes using the Lhasa Apso to protect their valuable wares. Doubtless the breed's inborn instinct to give a warning bark has been put to many a good use.

Lhasa Apsos were very valuable in the eyes of the Tibetans and were never sold. They were only given as gifts, as they were considered a talisman and were often presented as gifts for safe passage when travelling on the difficult and treacherous route from Tibet into China. This journey, by caravan, took from eight to 10 months to complete. They were certainly presented to the Imperial families of China

throughout the Manchu Dynasty, which lasted from 1583 until 1908. Among other notable personages, His Holiness the Dalai Lama had a custom of presenting Lhasa Apsos as bringers of good fortune.

Many Lhasa Apsos were very carefully bred and were jealously guarded by the Buddhist monks, who selected them with great care and took trouble to look after them well. However, there were undoubtedly occasions when Lhasa Apsos were crossed with other small Tibetan breeds. This is one of the reasons why the very occasional Apso puppy turns out to be a 'Prapso', looking more like a Tibetan Spaniel – a throwback to earlier times. The breed has no particular religious significance, as some have said, but certainly has a very close association with

THEORIES REGARDING THE NAME

Although, as I have previously explained, the word Apso (Apsok) can refer to any long-coated dog, it is used mainly with reference to the short-legged variety. One popular theory is that the word 'apso' is a derivation of 'rapso', which means 'goat-like' and we should keep in our minds that Tibetan goats are small with longer hair than those with which we are familiar in Britain. However, Tibetans say that it is only foreigners who have made this connection, and that, in any case, the word 'goat' in Tibetan is 'ra'. They agree, though, that the word 'apso' conjures up pictures of something shaggy-coated.

We also know that the breed was often called 'Apso Seng Kyi', or 'Bark Sentinel Lion Dog'. 'Ab' represents the noise of barking, 'seng' is 'lion' and 'kyi' is 'dog', but where did 'sentinel' creep in, I wonder? But when we also consider that 'sok' means 'hairy', I would venture to suggest that 'barking, hairy lion dog' is a closer representation of the truth.

There are so many wonderful stories about the mythical lion dog that there is not space to recount them all here, but one I would like to share with you is that of the lion's twisted curls. It is said that that the Buddha, who often rode on a mythical lion, remained so long in motionless contemplation that snails crawled over the lion's head.

We should also consider that the word 'Abso' (Asians frequently exchange the letters 'b' and 'p') has no literal meaning in the Tibetan language, but is a Mongolian word meaning 'wholly covered with hair all over', leading us to question whether the breed may in fact be of Mongolian origin further back in time.

Wherever our thoughts lead us as to the true origin of the breed, we can never doubt that the Lhasa Apso we know and so love today has very strong links with the 'lion dog' and Kylin, found in so many different forms throughout Tibet and the Far East.

the Buddhist faith. Even the present Dalai Lama, the 14th, had a black Lhasa Apso when he was young, and of this he was very fond.

COMING TO THE WEST

The Lhasa Apso was not only held in high esteem in the monasteries, it was, and still is, held in high regard by many and has always been carefully guarded and protected by its loving owners. This has meant that it has been very difficult for outsiders to acquire the breed and to bring it to the West, for monks and other owners of this very special breed have always been reluctant to part with their dogs.

Not all of them, though, lived a luxurious life. In 1906 we read of one that was purchased out of a Bhuteer's market cart. He was said to be "unkempt, unwashed, uninviting, and loath to be civilised." However, when we read these lines we must appreciate that Tibetan standards of cleanliness are far removed from our own and that this little dog, who valiantly guarded his vegetables, was most probably very highly prized by his tradesman owner. Clearly the

Apso who guarded this cart had a highly typical temperament for he was by no means friendly, and was quite prepared to protect his goods and chattels to grim death. This dog was one of the few who were allowed to leave Tibet; he was ultimately destined for the show ring and became known as Kepwick Tuko.

Another Apso who came into England from Tibet had an attendant covered in turquoises but, of course, Tibetans always like to wear their wealth when travelling, so this was not really unusual. Yet another Apso who made his way out of his homeland was reported to have been carried across the saddle for miles and miles.

An early importer of several foreign breeds was the Hon Mrs McLaren-Morrison who owned several Lhasa Apsos during the late 19th century. One of high renown was Bhutan, who became particularly well known because he begged at dog shows to raise money for the War Fund. Princess Alexandra, who was a regular visitor to shows, was heard to remark that dear little Bhutan looked as if he was begging to leave the show. Sadly, he contracted distemper and "died at his post, so to speak", according to his loving owner. This remarkable little fellow kept his end up to the very last, but kept sinking into a sitting position and finally went home to die.

ASSOCIATED BREEDS

We should also bear in mind that there are other breeds of dog indigenous to Tibet, some of them closely related to the Apso. The reason we need to consider them now is that when the breed finally arrived in the West, there was considerable confusion among some of them, about which we shall read more later.

TIBETAN TERRIER

The Tibetan Terrier we know so well in the West is clearly distinguishable from the Lhasa Apso, for it is substantially longer in the leg, standing 36-41 cms (14-16 ins) at the shoulder, and has a square outline. The foreface is also substantially longer than that of the Lhasa Apso and its

The Tibetan Terrier is a substantially bigger dog than the Lhasa Apso.
© Carol Ann Johnson

The Tibetan Spaniel has a much shorter coat than the Apso.
© Carol Ann Johnson

bite is usually scissor, though may be a reverse scissor. Like the Lhasa Apso, the long coat may be of any colour but, as with the Apso, a black nose is required by the Breed Standard, so that liver and chocolate coat colours are not acceptable in the show ring, although they exist in the Himalaya.

TIBETAN SPANIEL
Unlike the Tibetan Terrier, the Tibetan Spaniel has been fairly clearly defined as a separate breed from the Lhasa Apso since it first arrived in Britain in the late 19th century. Although the same height, weight varies between 4 and 7 kgs (9-15 lbs). This breed has a much shorter coat and is smooth on the face and on the front of the legs. Like the Lhasa Apso, this is not a square breed, but there is a marked difference in the forelegs, which are slightly bowed, and the Tibetan Spaniel should have hare feet, unlike those of the Apso. The shape of the skull also differs, that of the Tibetan Spaniel being slightly domed.

TIBETAN MASTIFF
The Tibetan Mastiff is the only large Tibetan breed we currently find in Britain and although it may not be obvious to the eye, it is likely that both this breed and the Lhasa Apso had common ancestors. This large, powerful dog should stand at least 66 cms (26 ins) at the shoulder if male, and at least 61 cms (24 ins) for a female. Weight is not given in the Breed Standard but tends to range between 45.5 kgs to 63.5 kgs (100-140 lbs).

This breed is used in Tibet to guard flocks from animals of prey, and is also invariably chained outside tents and homesteads as a means of protection. In Tibet this majestic animal was usually black and tan, black, or sometimes red, but slate grey is now also accepted in Britain. Interestingly, Tibetan Mastiffs with tan markings above the eyes are known as 'four eyes', something highly prized by Tibetans, as they are believed to be able to see evil three days in advance. In many countries this breed is known as 'Do Kyi', meaning 'dog you can tie up'.

Despite the difference in size, the Tibetan Mastiff and the Lhasa Apso share a common ancestry.

There are significant differences between the Shih Tzu and its close cousin, the Lhasa Apso.

KYI APSO

The Kyi Apso is another of Tibet's large dog breeds and is found principally in the region of Mount Kailash, in the south west of the country. This very rare breed was traditionally used by nomads to protect their livestock. In some ways they are similar to the Tibetan Mastiff but are rather smaller in frame, weighing roughly 34 to 41 kgs (75-90 lbs). The breed is notable for its bearded face.

TIBETAN HUNTING DOG OR SHA-KYI

Another breed we do not have in Britain is the Sha-Kyi, a dog used to kill game; he is taken to within sight of the game and then slipped. Roughly the size of an Airedale Terrier, he is generally creamy grey in colour, with a thick, short coat. They are fierce, due in part to the fact that the puppies are tied to their dams and dragged along when out hunting.

SHIH TZU

Although the Shih Tzu is not strictly a Tibetan breed, it is important to be aware of this, the Lhasa Apso's Sino-Tibetan cousin, for there has been certain confusion over the two breeds for many a long year. To the uninitiated, the Shih Tzu looks similar in outward appearance to the Lhasa Apso, with its long flowing coat and similar size, which should not exceed 27 cms (10.5 ins). However, there are many differences, both in construction and in the head (which is broad, round and wide between the eyes). This breed also has a very different personality and is usually friendly to everyone it meets.

EARLY YEARS IN BRITAIN

Although the various Tibetan breeds are now clearly defined, this has not always been the case. We learn from Colonel Duncan,

India, owned by the Hon Mrs McLaren-Morrison, was a son of Bhutan (who used to beg for charity at shows) , a male imported from the Himalaya by the same owner and registered with the Kennel Club in 1896. India was a highly acclaimed black and white dog, with dark, expressive eyes. In 1907 he was described as "typical of the breed" and "perhaps the best of the breed seen hitherto in England".

A Lhasa Apso bred by the Hon Mrs McLaren-Morrison and owned by Majorie Wild, pictured in 1906. This dog lived to be 18 years old.

in his charming book *Tomu From Tibet*, that the earliest Lhasa Apso known in England was brought here in 1854. Before the turn of the 20th century the dogs we now know as Lhasa Apsos and Tibetan Terriers were called by various names, among them Thibetan, Kashmir Bhutan, Bhuteer or Lhassa Terriers and even Thibet Poodles. To add to the confusion, puppies from the same litter were sometimes registered under different breed names. Clearly as two different breeds at that time came under the same 'umbrella', there were great discrepancies in size, some described as being as small as

Maltese Terriers, others as large as Russian Poodles.

Although there was a difference in size and in coat, something all the Tibetan dogs had in common was that their tails curled over their backs. In 1904 the Hon Mrs McLaren-Morrison said she felt much more attention should be paid to size, as the Tibetans paid great importance to this aspect. She believed there should be two classes, over and under a certain weight, but she did not specify what she felt that dividing weight should be. However, at that time most authorities described the weight range as only 8 to 15 lbs, which is just less than 4 kgs, up

to about 7.5 kgs.

By 1908 the breed had gained Championship status and was shown in two sizes, in different classes, so the breed we now know as the Tibetan Terrier was accommodated too. One of the earliest Champions in the breed was Ch. Rupso, who 'lives on' to this day, as his body is stuffed and now resides in the British Museum at Tring. He is labelled 'Tibetan Terrier', but he is most certainly an Apso, measuring 25 cms (almost 10 ins) at the shoulder.

Miss Marjorie Wild, of the famous Cotsvale affix, had her first Apso in 1900 or 1901. She

Taktru and Droma: Mrs Irma Bailey imported these two dogs into England from Tibet in 1928. Both were later owned by Mrs Dudley.

recalled seeing many beautiful and true-to-type specimens at pre-1914 shows, and these comments referred to the Lhasa Apso we know today. The Apso of those early years in Britain were mostly blue-black and white, all black, or varying shades of grey, including grizzle.

Sadly, as was the case for most breeds, during the First World War (1914-1918) the Lhassa Terrier, as it was known then, struggled to survive and little was heard of it until the late 1920s. The Hon. Mrs Irma Bailey had spent some time in Tibet, as her husband was involved in the Younghusband Expedition in 1904 and took over from Sir Charles Bell as Political Officer for Tibet in 1921. She stated quite openly that "the long-legged dogs shown in this country would not be admired in Tibet".

Mrs Bailey came into close contact with many Tibetan nobles and made extensive enquiries about the breed. She found that apart from being a small dog, it must have a long coat, "the longer the better, within reason". She acquired her first two dogs, Sengtru and Apso, while living in Sikkim, on the Tibetan frontier. These dogs had originally been given to Sir Charles Bell's medical officer, Colonel Kennedy, by Tsarong Shape, who was Commander-in-Chief. When Colonel Kennedy retired from service in 1922, he presented his two dogs to Mrs Bailey.

Each time Mrs Bailey and her husband went into Tibet, they took with them their two dogs and tried hard to find others of the same kind. It appears they could easily find similar dogs, but they wanted "the same type in all particulars, including especially colour". These dogs were gold, for Mrs Bailey had been told that the Tibetans preferred a golden or honey-coloured dog for this resembled the lion. (What had not been appreciated at that time was that the lion to which the Tibetans liken the breed is actually the mythical Snow Lion, which is white.)

The Baileys' search proved impossible, but in 1934 Colonel Bailey spent a month in Lhasa

Lhasa Apsos and their proud owners pictured at an early show.

and was in frequent contact with His Holiness The Dalai Lama. Through His Holiness and other high officials he continued his search and eventually found a black bitch belonging to a young Tibetan officer. Although the officer would not agree to part with the bitch, he allowed Colonel Bailey to take her away to breed from. The Baileys knew that new blood was essential to develop their strain, for until then they had only bred from their original pair. The black bitch was also named 'Apso', so she was renamed 'Demon' and was mated to Sengtru, producing a litter of puppies. Sadly, when Demon was sent back to Tibet, she was lost *en route* and was never seen again.

The breed was exhibited in 1929, but there was enormous confusion due to the great disparity between the Tibetan dogs. It was clear to everyone that two different 'types' of dog were being exhibited, but under the same breed name.

FURTHER CONFUSION IN THE 1930s

Mrs Bailey had imported Lhasa Terriers into Britain in 1928, but confusion was heightened a couple of years later when some dogs, known as 'Tibetan Lion Dogs', were imported from China by Miss Hutchins. Two of these were owned by General and Mrs Brownrigg, who were later to become Sir Douglas and Lady Brownrigg. It was already known

that Lhassa Terriers, now sometimes referred to as Lhasa Apsos, were given to distinguished people in China, and this probably played a large part in the assumption that these newly imported dogs were Lhasa Apsos.

When Lady Brownrigg returned to England in 1931, her dogs were carefully compared with those belonging to the Baileys, which had recently been imported from Tibet. The Tibetan dogs were found to have narrower heads, longer noses and smaller eyes than Lady Brownrigg's dogs. Despite this they were all shown alongside one another at the West of England Ladies Kennel Club Show in 1933. Only later was a division between them made.

TIBETAN BREEDS ASSOCATION

With the aim of drawing a distinction between the various dogs of Tibet, the Tibetan Breeds Association was established in 1934. This had initially been prompted by Mr A. Croxton-Smith, Chairman of the Kennel Club, who had approached Mrs Bailey with a request that the confusion be sorted out.

A meeting took place at Lady Freda Valentine's Green Street home in London and 'ideals' were set down. I had the great pleasure of knowing Lady Freda in her closing years and spent time with her in London, where she always amused me by recounting the events of that meeting and the many that followed. The situation was tense, but to bring some measure of calm she would ask the most difficult personality amongst those present to pass around the cream cakes, making her obliged to speak to everyone in the room, if only to ask them if they would like a cake!

The outcome was that four Tibetan breeds were officially accepted: the Lhasa Apso, the Tibetan Terrier, the Tibetan Spaniel and the Tibetan Mastiff. The Chinese dogs were named Shih Tzu and classified as a separate breed. Even in China there had been confusion between the breeds, but the Peking Kennel Club was formed in 1934 and Chinese Standards were also drawn up in 1938.

THE FIRST BREED STANDARD

The following is the original Lhasa Apso Breed Standard, as issued by the Tibetan Breeds Association in 1934:

'(In judging these dogs, breed characteristics are of paramount importance)

1. Character – Gay and assertive, but chary of strangers.
2. Size – Variable, but about 10 inches [25 cm] or 11 inches [28 cms] at shoulder for dogs, bitches slightly smaller.
3. Colour – Golden, sandy, honey, dark grizzle, slate, smoke, particolour, black, white or brown. This being the true Tibetan Lion-dog, golden or lion-like colours are preferred. Other colours in order as above. Dark tips to ears and beard are an asset.
4. Body Shape – The length from point of shoulder to point of buttocks longer then height at withers, well ribbed up, strong loin, well-developed quarters and thighs.
5. Coat – Heavy, straight, hard, not woolly or silky, of good length and very dense.
6. Mouth and Muzzle – Mouth level, otherwise slightly undershot preferable. Muzzle of medium length; a square muzzle is objectionable.
7. Head – Heavy head furnishings with good fall over eyes, good whiskers and beard; skull narrow, falling away behind the eyes in a marked degree, not quite flat, but not domed or apple-shaped; straight foreface of fair length. Nose black, about 1½ inches [38 mm] long, or the length from tip of nose to eye to be roughly one-third of the total length from nose to back of skull.
8. Eyes – Dark brown, neither very large and full, nor very small and sunk.

Breed enthusiasts were determined to create a Breed Standard that would mark the Lhasa Aspo as a distinct breed.

9. Ears – Pendant, heavily feathered.
10. Legs – Forelegs straight; both fore and hind legs heavily furnished with hair.
11. Feet – Well feathered, should be round and cat-like with good pads.
12. Tail and Carriage – Well feathered, should be carried well over back in a screw; there may be a kink at the end. A low carriage of stern is a serious fault.'

Although the Lhasa Apso had now found a firm footing, with interest in the breed being on the increase, only 12 were entered at Crufts in 1935, indicating that they were still not widely known.

THE LHASA APSO ARRIVES IN AMERICA
In the first month of the Water Bird Year, which was early in 1933, His Holiness the 13th Dalai Lama, sent a gift of two Lhasa Apsos to Mr and Mrs Suydam Cutting in the United States. The Cuttings had seen Mrs Bailey's Apsos in Nepal and had also set up a 'correspondence friendship' with His Holiness – indeed they had already sent him two Dalmatians and two 'German Hounds'.

After the death of the 13th Dalai Lama a further two Apsos were sent to the Cuttings, and then two more, in 1950, by the 14th Dalai Lama. These last two were Le and Phema, who both became American Champions. The bitch, Phema, sadly had no puppies, but Le sired several litters. It was largely thanks to the Cuttings, and their world-renowned Hamilton kennel, that the Lhasa Apso found its place on the American show scene.

Others who played important roles in the establishment of the breed in America were the Lloyds of New Jersey and Miss Daisy Frazier whose Lost Horizon kennel was in California.

A CASE OF FALSE IDENTITY
In 1934, a Lhasa Apso was exhibited at a show in New York under the breed name of Lhassa Terrier, and an American Breed Standard was drawn up in 1935. Unfortunately, great confusion arose in the USA and this has had a long-term detrimental effect on the breed across the world.

Between 1937 and 1950 some dogs were imported to America, and were registered, in good faith, as Lhasa Apsos. But by the time their true identity was recognised, they had already been bred from. They were actually Shih Tzu! As a result, the Shih Tzu is behind many Lhasa Apso pedigrees, and with the movement of dogs across the globe, this has affected the breed in many different countries.

When tracing pedigrees back, it is possible to see where the unintentional crosses were made in America, and, as a result, it is possible to calculate the percentage of Shih Tzu blood that lies behind particular Lhasa Apsos. Thankfully, some American lines remained clear during that confused period through to 1950.

THE SECOND WORLD WAR YEARS

The war years created enormous problems for all dog breeds in Britain, and many struggled to survive. A great many dogs were destroyed, their owners preferring to know the end of their favourites, rather than being put in the position of having to find them other homes with strangers. The Kennel Club asked people to breed as few litters as possible, something many breeders considered rather premature, particularly bearing in mind that many dogs had already been destroyed.

Thelma Gray wrote a report in the dog press in March 1940, expressing her concern that, for the lesser-known breeds, including the Tibetan breeds, this was a real crisis. There was much debate over the general situation in the canine press, and people were at pains to prove that dogs could be fed on foodstuffs that did not deprive human beings, who were so severely rationed.

Between 1939 and 1944, Mrs Bailey registered only five dogs with the Kennel Club, and Miss Wild also registered five; hers came from two litters, both by the same sire. How dreadfully sad it was that Miss Wild's strain was completely wiped out in the late 1940s, due to a severe attack of hardpad and distemper. But Dr and Mrs Greig, two ladies well known for their Tibetan Terriers,

After the Second World War, there was still time to import a handful of dogs from Tibet. © *Juliette Cunliffe*

also produced some Lhasa Apsos, descended from two of the Baileys' imports, Lhasa and Litsi.

By the time the war drew to its close, Lhasa Apso bloodlines had dwindled dramatically and the breed was very thin on the ground. Clearly the breed had to be built up once again, and, thankfully, there was still time to import a handful of dogs from Tibet before the Chinese finally banned all movement of dogs out of the country. These imports, though, were largely of unknown pedigree. Lt. Col. and Mrs H.V. Irwin (Madamswood) imported a dog and a bitch in 1946. These they mated together in 1947 and 1948, producing two litters. Another import came in from India in 1948; this was Lady

Doreen Hope's Hopetoun Figaro, and Mrs P. Leigh imported the bitch, Tika Rant, from Tibet in 1948. The following year saw five imports from India, and Lady Doreen Hope, who had now become Lady Doreen Prior-Palmer, imported Hamilton Tura from the Cuttings in the USA.

As the 1950s emerged, registrations increased slightly, largely thanks to the Madamswood kennel and Miss Hervey-Cecil's Furzyhurst breeding. Later Mrs Flo Dudman's Ramblersholt's dogs came to the fore, as did the Brackenbury dogs, owned by Miss Beryl Harding, who was later to become Mrs Beryl Prince.

A BREED APART

All this while the Lhasa Apso had been included as one of the breeds looked after by the Tibetan Breeds Association, which had been set up in 1934. In 1956 Apso breeders felt their breed had become strong enough to break away and form a breed-specific club. By December of that same year, the Kennel Club had given its approval for the Lhasa Apso Club to be formed. But fewer than half of the club's membership of 27 actually had Apsos of their own.

Under the chairmanship of Irma Bailey, the club began by holding its show in conjunction with the Ladies Kennel Association. The only other shows at which breed classes were scheduled were the West of England Ladies Kennel Society, and Crufts.

As the Lhasa Apso was the only one of the Tibetan breeds that did not have 'Tibetan' as part of its name, in 1959 the breed name was changed to Tibetan Apso. But this lasted only a decade and in 1970 it was again changed back to Lhasa Apso.

By 1964, the breed was on a sound enough footing for the Kennel Club to re-issue Challenge Certificates. In May of that year they confirmed that there would be an allocation of nine sets of Certificates for the following year, beginning with Crufts 1965.

Ch. Brackenbury Gunga Din of Verles: The breed's first post-war Champion.

THE BREED'S FIRST CHAMPION

After Championship status was restored in Britain, Brackenbury Gunga Din of Verles was the first Lhasa Apso to gain the coveted title of Champion. This great day came at West of England Ladies' Kennel Association (WELKS) in 1965, under judge Marjorie Wild (Cotsvale). Although Gunga Din had won well on the show circuit during the previous five years, he was seven years old when he won his crown.

Sired by Jigmey Tharkay of Rungit and out of Brackenbury Min-nee, he was bred by Miss Beryl Harding on 18 December 1958 and was transferred to the ownership of Mr and Mrs F.J. Hesketh-Williams in 1959.

CH. GUNGA DIN'S SIRE

Ch. Brackenbury Gunga Din of Verles' sire, Jigmey Tharkay of Rungit, had been given to Mrs Jill Henderson by Sherpa Tenzin Norgay of Everest fame. His date of birth and pedigree were unknown, but he was imported from Darjeeling in India and, although there had been confusion over the name for a while, was registered with the English Kennel Club in March 1957. He did not remain in Britain for long, later living in Peru and in South Africa, where he died tragically at the age of 16, following an injury by guard dogs. However, his legacy lives on through his famous son and his name can be traced back behind many of today's Lhasa Apsos.

BREED PIONEERS

The Hon. Mrs McLaren-Morrison played an important part in the establishment of many foreign breeds in Britain, including the Lhasa Apso. In her day she was the acknowledged authority on Central Asiatic dogs. In 1896 she imported Bhutan from the Himalaya, and, amongst several Lhasa Apsos she owned, one was Ch. Little Dargee. Mrs McLaren-Morrison was the earliest-known exponent of the breed in Britain.

Sir Lionel Jacob was an expert in Indian dogs and was in government service in the Punjab. He had sufficient interest in what he called the 'Llassa Terrier' to draw up an unofficial Breed Standard in 1901. Even then he was clearly of the

SIR LIONEL JACOB'S 1901 DESCRIPTION OF THE BREED

Head. Distinctly terrier-like. Skull narrow, falling away behind the eyes in a marked degree, not quite flat, but not domed or apple-shaped. Fore-face of fair length, strong in front of the eyes, the nose large and prominent and pointed, not depressed, a square muzzle is objectionable. The stop size for size about that of a Skye terrier. Mouth quite level, but of the two a slightly overshot mouth is preferable to an undershot one. The teeth are somewhat smaller than would be expected in a terrier of the size. In this respect the breed seems to suffer to an extraordinary degree from cankered teeth. I have never yet seen an imported specimen with a sound mouth.

Ears. Set on low, and carried close to the cheeks, similar to the ears of a drop-eared Skye.

Eyes. Neither very large and full, nor very small and sunk, dark brown in colour.

Legs and Feet. The forelegs should be straight. In all short-legged breeds there is a tendency to crookedness, but the straighter the legs the better. There should be good bone. Owing to the heavy coat the legs look, and should look, heavy in bone; but in reality the bone is not heavy. It should be round and of good strength right down to the toes, the less ankle the better. The hocks should be particularly well let down. Feet should be round and cat-like with good pads.

Body. There is a tendency in England to look for a level top and a short back. All the best specimens have a slight arch at the loin, and the back should not be too short; it should be considerably longer than height at withers. The dog should be well ribbed up with a strong loin, and well developed thighs.

Stern. Should be well carried over the back after the manner of the tail of the Chow. All Thibetan dogs carry their tails in this way, and a low carriage of tail is a sign of impure blood.

Coat. Should be heavy, of good length and very dense. There should be a strong growth on the skull, falling on both sides. The legs should be well-clothed right down to the toes. On the body the hair should not reach to the ground, as in a show Yorkshire; there should be a certain amount of daylight. In general appearance the hair should convey the idea of being much harder to the eye than it is to the touch. It should look hard, straight, and strong, when to the touch it is soft, but not silky. The hair should always be straight, with no tendency to curl.

Colour. Black, dark grizzle, slate, sandy, or admixture of these colours with white.

Size. About 10 ins or 11 ins [25-28 cms] height at shoulder for dogs, and 9 ins or 10 ins [23-25 cms] for bitches.

opinion that the breed should be accepted as a distinct one, and that it should be recognised by the Kennel Club.

The description of the breed (see panel), which he wrote over a century ago, makes an interesting comparison with the standard we use today:

Although Miss Marjorie Wild (Cotsvale) owned Apsos from around the turn of the century, she did not begin showing and breeding until 1914, continuing her active involvement in the breed until her death in 1971. How sad it was that she was unable to fulfil her lifelong ambition to judge at Crufts in 1971, when she was already suffering ill health.

Lieutenant Colonel Eric Bailey and the Hon Mrs Irma Bailey, as we have already read, played an integral part in establishing the breed in Britain. Although we have already learned much about their dogs, horticulturalists will be interested to know that it was Lt. Col. Bailey who discovered the Blue Poppy, which was named after him as *Meconopsis baileyi*. He also joined Captain Morshead in charting an authoritative map of Tibet.

Irma Bailey had been a good friend of Lady Freda Valentine since they were girls, and in 1933 gave her an Apso dog, Chang-Tru, as a wedding gift. The Hon. Mrs Bailey outlived her husband by 21

Lady Freda Valentine's Chang-Tru, one of the breed's early exhibits.

years and died at the age of 92 in 1988.

Lady Freda Valentine CBE was involved with Apsos from the early 1930s and retained her interest though her long life of 93 years, dying on 10 January 1989. She had played host to many a meeting regarding the formation of the Tibetan Breeds Association, and again when the Lhasa Apso Club (LAC) was set up in 1956. She was on the LAC's Committee from its formation and following a long Vice-Presidency, was appointed President in 1987. She had a keen interest in all the Tibetan breeds, while her sister, Lady Vivien Younger, had a

Tibetan Mastiff. Lady Freda was also a Treasurer and Vice-President of Guide Dogs for the Blind.

Her beloved Chang-Tru was among the early exhibits in the breed and she had a veritable storehouse of wonderful memories of him, every one of them told with a twinkle in her eye, which I shall always remember. She was particularly fond of a 'heart-shaped' tongue, and was particularly proud of this picture, which she so adored.

Mrs Daisy Greig and Dr A.R.H. Greig are two notable ladies now best known for their Tibetan Terriers, which they bred under their Ladkok and Lamleh affixes, but they also helped to keep alive the line of Mrs Bailey's imported Lhasa Apsos. Some of her theories on the breed were rather extraordinary, and I have not included them in the history of the breed, having been unable to substantiate them.

Major Scott Cockburn owned a grey and white dog, Dzong-Pon, and a golden bitch, Pamo. These were presented to him by His Holiness The Dalai Lama and were registered with the English Kennel Club in 1934. These Apsos were successful in the show ring and provided useful fresh bloodlines, as they were unrelated to other dogs in Britain, and to each other, when they were imported.

Sherpa Tenzing Norgay with his Apsos.

Florence Dudman (Ramblersholt), although breeding only on a small scale, helped to keep the breed alive during the years following the Second World War. She generally kept males and bred in conjunction with Miss Hervey-Cecil (Furzyhurst), who kept bitches. They managed to retain some lines going back to Ladkok and Lamleh breeding.

Tenzing Norgay is best known as Sherpa Tenzing (sometimes spelt Tenzin) who climbed Everest with Sir Edmund Hillary in 1953. A life-long animal lover, he was given two Apsos by Tibetan monks and was made to promise that he would not part with them; one he named Ghangar and the other, Tasang. He took both to Darjeeling where he founded a kennel and retained a keen interest in the breed, which was always evident when he visited the UK.

Jill Henderson had been given two Apsos by Tenzing Norgay when she was Secretary to the Himalayan Climbing Club in Darjeeling. These were Ang Lhamo and Jigmey Tharkay of Rungit who, as we have already learned, was the sire of Britain's first post-war Champion.

Ms Beryl Harding (Brackenbury) joined the Tibetan Breeds Association in 1951 and was elected to its Committee the following year. The next year she looked after Colonel and Mrs Irwin's Dzongpen and Minzong of Madamswood. She was allowed to mate them and keep all but one of the puppies, which she did. One of the puppies was Brackenbury Lhotse, who won well in the show ring before Challenge Certificates

were on offer and was to become the grand-dam of Ch. Brackenbury Gunga Din of Verles. Miss Harding's bitch, Brackenbury Chigi-Gyemo, also became a Champion in 1965.

In 1977 Beryl Harding married her life-long friend, Colonel Prince, who gave many years to the Lhasa Apso Club as Treasurer. They are both sorely missed by those of us who knew them.

THE MODERN ERA

It is always difficult to know where one era ends and another starts, but 1965 was certainly a landmark year with the restoration of those all-important Challenge Certificates, three of which, awarded by different judges, allow a dog to attain the coveted title of Champion.

It was Daphne Hesketh Williams who had the honour of winning the first such accolade with Gunga Din. She was breed note correspondent for *Dog World* for many a long year and served as Hon. Secretary of the Lhasa Apso Club for 21 years, the only people having held this post following her being Margot Cook, myself (Juliette Cunliffe) and Graham Holmes.

Daphne Hesketh-Williams campaigned her dogs actively during the 1960s and 1970s, making up a number of Champions in the UK, with others of her breeding gaining their titles abroad. Her last British Champion was Belazieth's Ja of Verles, bred by Rob and Doreen Richardson in 1971, and gaining her title in 1975.

Thelma Morgan became involved with Lhasa Apsos around the same time as Daphne Hesketh-Williams and was breed note correspondent for the other weekly canine newspaper, *Our Dogs*. She was very interested in colour genetics and played a large part in reviving the Bhuteer particolours through descendents of Conquistador Kismet. Her Ffrith affix, however, was not always used in her breeding. Thelma Morgan's first Champion, Namista Yarsi, bred by Mr and Mrs Lord, gained his 'crown' in 1965. Mrs Morgan's daughter, Glenis Dolphin, was involved with the Lhasa Apso from childhood and has carried on her mother's interest in the breed as well as successfully breeding and campaigning Shih Tzu.

By now numbers in the breed were building up rapidly and many new breeders and enthusiasts had joined the ranks. Indeed, the breed moved on so fast that it would not be possible to pay due tribute to the many people who have played an important role in the past half century, but there some who cannot go without mention, for their breeding has formed a cornerstone of the breed.

Mrs Anne Matthews' Hardacre breeding has made a great mark on the breed, as she has campaigned a veritable wealth of Champions over the years, starting with her foundation bitch, Ch. Tungwei of Coburg, who became a Champion in 1968. Rob and Doreen Richardson's first Apso was Hardacre Gloria of Belazieth, a

Juliette Cunliffe pictured on the balcony of her home in Nepal, with Lama Nirmal Gurung, Lama Gopal Gurung Rinpoche, and her three Apsos Chenpo, Kitty and Lhamo.
© *Dibya Baral*

daughter of Gunga Din, and who produced the Richardson's first Champion, Belazieth's Salt 'n' Pepper, who is to be found in the background of many notable pedigrees.

Jean Blyth's Saxonsprings kennel has also had a far-reaching impact on the breed, both at home and abroad. Perhaps her three most famous dogs are Ch./Am. Ch. Orlanes Intrepid, bred by co-owner Joan Kendall in the USA, and two of his many offspring, Ch. Saxonsprings Hackensack (who won Best in Show at Crufts in 1984), and the late great Ch. Saxonsprings Fresno (who became Pedigree Chum's Top Dog of the Year in 1982). Fresno was expertly campaigned by Geoff Corish and eventually transferred to his ownership, living with him until her death. Fresno

is still the breed recordholder in Lhasa Apsos, breaking the record held by Ch. Sternroc Alexander, a dog bred by Pamela Cross-Stern and co-owned by Francis Sefton.

So time has moved on and, with it, the success of our wonderful breed that regularly achieves high accolades among strong all-breed competition at Championship Shows. I hope our current successful breeders and exhibitors will forgive me for not mentioning them here, but to merely pay 'lip service' would not do them justice, and, were I to mention them all, this book would become a veritable tome. All of us, though, will be able to look back and see who was involved in those early years, helping the Lhasa Apso reach the heights of fame and success with which it is associated today.

A LHASA APSO FOR YOUR LIFESTYLE

Chapter 3

Taking on any breed of dog is a heavy commitment that must not be undertaken lightly. Taking on a Lhasa Apso carries with it even greater responsibility, due largely to the breed's long coat and also to its rather special temperament, which does not fit in with all family situations.

MAKING THE COMMITMENT

Hopefully by the time you are ready to make the commitment to have an Apso you will already have done an enormous amount of homework to be certain that this is really the right breed for you and your family.

You will have asked yourself whether you can devote sufficient time to an Apso's coat care, even if you have decided to keep him as a family pet rather than as a show dog, in which case you may

decide to trim the coat. This will ideally need to be done professionally, unless you are already a skilled groomer, so grooming costs must be taken into consideration, whether your Apso is for pet or for show.

The length and density of coat means there is a serious time commitment, which is very serious indeed if the coat is to be kept at full length. Although the Lhasa Apso does not shed his coat, the long coat and wet feet can cause a lot of extra housework after your dog has come running in from the garden on a winter's day.

There are, of course, always costs associated with dogs, but we shall look at these more specifically as we progress through this chapter.

WHO WILL LOOK AFTER YOUR DOG?

If you are a working person and

about to be an owner of a Lhasa Apso, you must seriously consider who will look after your dog while you are not at home. In this day and age, more and more people work from home – a situation that is ideal for Apso ownership. You can be assured that your Apso will keep you good company throughout the day; the only problem being that if you sit at a computer all day, as I do, there will almost always be an Apso reclining under your seat, running into the danger of your chair wheels rolling over the coat, removing clumps of hair!

If you work away from home on a full-time basis, you must be realistic and not take on the ownership of a dog unless you have someone responsible to look after it, at least a few hours each day. Any dog should be able to be left for two or three hours each day, but not any longer. It may be that a member of your household

This is a breed that thrives on human companionship. © *Juliette Cunliffe*

HOW MUCH DOES IT COST?

If you wish to buy a Lhasa Apso puppy with a good pedigree, expect to pay several hundred pounds. It may be slightly more if you aim to have a show dog rather than a pet, but both should have been raised to the same high standards, so there may not be a very great difference. It is probably best to ring a breed club secretary to get some advice on price before you start to make your enquiries. The secretary may also know who has puppies available at the time of your enquiry, so will be able to point you in the right direction.

It is imperative that you purchase from a reputable breeder. The Kennel Club now offers an Accredited Breeder Scheme, but there are many good and experienced breeders who choose not to take part in this for very valid reasons. On the other hand, there are several not-so-good breeders who, although 'Accredited', manage to slip through the net. You will really need to use your own intuitive powers when choosing a breeder. Make sure you ask the right questions, and expect to be asked many questions in return. Remember that bad breeders are often 'in it for the money', so you may well find them asking a high price for their stock, even though little thought has gone into the breeding, and probably little into the care of the puppies.

I have heard of so-called 'breeders' who have two litters of similarly aged puppies running

will be there while you are out at work, or a professional dog sitter or walker could probably be employed. But this, of course, will involve additional expense and the cost may be prohibitive if it is something that has to be done on a regular basis.

Some people are able to take their dogs to work with them and this could be a very good arrangement. But you must consider the personality of your particular Lhasa Apso and should not expect him necessarily to take to this arrangement without hesitation. If you do find yourself in this fortunate work situation, it is best to introduce your Apso to the routine while he still young. In this way, he should adapt more easily and will come to accept the people around him. But remember that all dogs, although they may enjoy the 'going to work' routine, must have frequent opportunities to go for short walks and to relieve themselves. Puppies, of course, need toilet breaks more often than adults. The last thing you want is for your dog to disgrace himself in the office – he may never be invited again!

around together with two dams, and the breeder has simply not known which puppies belong to which bitch. Now that is what I call a really bad breeder! If this happens, or if for any reason you are unsure, do not let your heart rule your head. Simply walk away, which may discourage the breeder from trying to earn money from producing litters.

When good breeders are setting a price for their puppies, they will have taken into consideration the many expenses they have incurred. These will include health checks on the dam prior to mating, a stud fee, which can be considerable when using a health-checked dog of high quality, veterinary costs that may have been involved prior to and post whelping, and possibly vaccination fees, at least for the first vaccine, this depending upon the age at which the puppies leave home. Added to this there will be Kennel Club registration fees, and it is certainly to be hoped that the puppy you buy will be KC registered. Puppies that are not KC registered will cost considerably less, but there will be a reason why this is the case, usually a negative one, so, as a purchaser, you will need an honest explanation.

You will also have to bear in mind the cost of your dog's upkeep. Apart from the grooming costs involved, there will also be the cost of food, veterinary bills and other incidentals, such as bedding, collars and leads, and maybe even a little coat to wear

The Lhasa Apso is a healthy breed, but veterinary bills, even for routine care, do mount up.

when out walking in inclement weather. You may decide to take out veterinary insurance, but this will not cover the cost of routine vaccinations or other preventative care.

FOOD

There are so very many different ways of feeding a dog, and the cost will depend on the type you choose. The Lhasa Apso is not a large breed, so costs are not so much as feeding a Deerhound or a Great Dane. Nonetheless, food costs do mount up over a year, and this should never be overlooked when calculating how much it will cost you to keep your dog.

For information on feeding a Lhasa Apso, see Chapter Five: The Best of Care.

EQUIPMENT
Food bowls, grooming equipment, collars, leads, bedding and even 'poo bags' all

If you are keeping your Apso in full coat, you will need to find space for a grooming room.

mount up. My advice is that any items that can be used long-term should be of the highest quality so that you get as much life out of them as possible. The initial outlay will be a little higher, but over time these will most probably turn out to be cost-saving. Stainless-steel feeding and water bowls, for example, don't cost much more than ceramic bowls, but apart from being much more hygienic, they will last almost forever.

TRAINING

Training need not cost money at all if you are able to train a dog yourself, but you may want to take your Apso along to training classes – ringcraft for a show dog and obedience for a pet. Most of these classes are very inexpensive, but there are also some private training establishments, which

cost more. Most of these run six-, eight-, or 10-week courses, for which you have to pay a course fee.

Some training classes help dogs to work toward the Kennel Club Good Citizen scheme, in which there are bronze, silver and gold awards. These make very good sense and provide evidence that your Apso is indeed a 'Good Citizen'.

If you have difficulty with your Apso's temperament or encounter other behavioural problems, you may decide on a one-to-one training situation, which will be much more costly. But remember, you must be trained as well as your dog, so please don't send your dog away for training. This simply won't work long-term, and when your dog returns home you will almost certainly be back at square one again!

Other forms of training include agility, obedience and heelwork to music.

For more information, see Chapter Six: Training and Behaviour.

VETERINARY BILLS

Bear in mind that the Lhasa Apso is a long-lived breed, and veterinary costs are likely to rise during the closing years of your dog's life. Sometimes Lhasa Apsos get 'dry eye' when they get into their teens, so the eye needs to be kept artificially moist. In mild cases, artificial 'tear drops' may be sufficient to keep the problem at bay, but in more severe cases a special tube of liquid is needed from your vet. Just for the sake of example, as this book goes to press I have to pay over £40 per tube for a 16-year-old Apso, and this lasts less than a month, so be warned: your veterinary bills can easily creep upward as time goes on.

INSURANCE

Insurance is not an inexpensive item by any means and will run easily into three figures each year. Price usually depends on the size of the dog, so an Apso tends to be at the lower end of the price scale. If you have only one dog, or perhaps a couple, insurance is an extremely good idea, but do shop around to see which companies offer the best deals. Remember, too, that the cheapest is not always the best.

Usually you will still have to pay for minor treatment and generally an excess of the first

£30 or so for more costly work by your vet. You are asked to put in a claim for treatment and the cheque will come through a while later, some sooner than others. Insurance policies also usually cover third-party injury, or damage to someone else's property. As Lhasa Apsos are not hunting dogs and not large enough to cause too much damage, with luck, you will never have to claim for these, but it's always reassuring to keep in the back of your mind should the unforeseen happen!

GROOMING

As a Lhasa Apso is the breed you have chosen, grooming will be highly important part of canine maintenance and will involve cost in terms of money and time, especially the latter.

This means you will need to set aside a place in the home for grooming. If you have a utility room off your kitchen, this is probably ideal. Obviously there will be a considerable outlay in terms of equipment, but if you keep your Apso in short coat, usually known as 'pet trim', you will cut down on these costs a little, although you will most probably have professional grooming bills, which will mount up.

When selecting a professional groomer for your Apso, do make sure they understand the breed and have suitable experience. There may be a parlour to which you can take your pet, but some operate a mobile service so they bath and groom your Apso in your own home, which you and your dog may prefer.

THE RIGHT PUPPY

Hopefully, the Lhasa Apso who joins you will be Kennel Club registered, and his breeder will be a member of at least one of the Lhasa Apso breed clubs, indicating that she abides by the club's code of ethics. If you wish to show your Apso, it is essential that the puppy is KC registered and the price will reflect this. As I have already said, many not-so-good breeders whose puppies are not registered still charge high prices, but an unregistered puppy should be considerably less.

DOG OR BITCH?

We have already discussed some of the differences between dogs and bitches, but which you choose is really a matter of personal preference. Within each litter, dogs tend to be a little larger than bitches. When they have reached maturity, dogs lift their legs, while bitches squat to do their toilet. From a practical point of view, the gardeners among you may favour your flower beds over a pristine lawn, or vice versa!

I have owned the breed for over 30 years now, and, thinking back, it has generally tended to be the dogs that are the more affectionate, but there have

Choosing a female (left) or a male (right) comes down to personal preference.

certainly been exceptions. I have one especially devoted bitch at the moment who always creeps up over my shoulder when I am reading a book in bed at night. Soon enough her head is pressed firmly under my chin, so that I can no longer see the pages of my book, but she is loved all the more for this slight inconvenience.

As dogs reach maturity they are usually ready to pursue any bitch that happens to be in season. An Apso's interest in this regard can even commence from the age of seven months and I have known of litters that have been produced as the result of such unexpected encounters. So if you have a male Apso, never underestimate his sexual desires and prowess! Bitches, on the other hand, are usually only receptive to males for roughly four days at the height of their season; the rest of the time they will make it clear they are not ready for his desires. Leading up to a season, and also afterwards, a bitch's hormones affect her mood, and I find Apsos can be rather temperamental at these times, especially with other bitches.

If you have both sexes in your canine family, there must be some sort of provision for the two to be kept apart when your bitch is in season. If you have more than one bitch, keep in mind that when one is in season, she will often 'bring the other/s in', so at least you will be able to get the difficult time over in a relatively short while. After this, household life can return to its usual blissful normality.

FINDING A BREEDER

The obvious first port of call when you begin to look for a Lhasa Apso puppy is to contact the secretary of one of the specialist breed clubs, either the one that is most local to you, or the 'parent' club, which serves the whole country (in Britain this is the Lhasa Apso Club). Contact details change from time to time, so if you have difficulty knowing where to find details, I suggest you call the Kennel Club. If you have access to the internet, most clubs have their own website, so if you just type in 'Lhasa Apso' and scroll down, you will find the clubs listed.

The secretaries of clubs will generally be able to put you in touch with breeders who have litters or who have bitches due to whelp very soon. The advantage of speaking to a breed club secretary is that they know and understand the breed, and have at least some knowledge of who the breeders are. Seeking advice through a less-specialised source does not have this advantage.

Be aware that breeders will not usually allow you to view the puppies at a very young age, probably not until they are four weeks or older, when their eyes are open and they are starting to walk around and play. However anxious you may be to see your potential new puppy, don't be over-anxious, for unless you are an experienced breeder, you are unlikely to know what traits you should be looking for in a young whelp. Under no circumstances should you arrange to collect a

You will not be allowed to view puppies when they are very young, but you can start making enquiries about the litter. *© Juliette Cunliffe*

QUESTIONS TO ASK THE BREEDER

You will have questions to ask when you make initial telephone enquiries to a breeder, and doubtless more still if and when you decide to visit the litter. But before taking the decision to travel to meet the breeder and her dogs, you should ascertain that this is indeed a likely litter from which you wish to choose a puppy.

- Is the litter Kennel Club registered?

- Have the sire and dam been tested for progressive retinal atrophy (PRA)? If so, you must ask to see the certificates when you visit.

- Are the parents show dogs or pets?

- What breeding are the puppies and what lines do they carry? Ask also if both parents will be available to see or, if the sire is owned by someone else, if a photo will be available or can perhaps be viewed online.

- If the parents are show dogs, what major awards have they won?

- How many puppies were born in the litter, and how many are still available for sale?

- What sex are the puppies that are available?

- What colours are available?

- How old are the pups now, and when would they be ready to leave?

- Has the litter been raised in the home or in a kennel situation?

- Have they been well socialised, and have they yet met any children?

- Will the puppies have been fully or partially vaccinated before they leave, and will this be included in the price?

- Will puppies be microchipped?

- Will any restrictions be placed on their Kennel Club registrations?

- What is the price?

- Will the breeder continue to offer advice throughout the dog's life, and would she take the Apso back should unforeseen circumstances arise?

puppy that is less than eight weeks old. Many good breeders do not allow their puppies to leave until they are about 10 weeks, but eight is the absolute minimum.

When visiting a litter it is unlikely that the puppies' sire will be available for you to see, unless he is owned by the breeder. But, in any event, you should be able to see a photograph of him. If the breeder has a website, you may also be able to view pictures of the puppies, their dam and possibly their sire on the internet, which will give you some idea of colouring at least.

VIEWING THE LITTER
First of all, I would like to stress that you must be honest with both the breeder and yourself. If you try to cover up some important facts about your own home situation, you may end up with the wrong puppy out of the litter, or indeed a Lhasa Apso

It is important to see the puppies' mother to find out the looks and temperament they are likely to inherit.

Spend time watching the puppies so you get an idea of their individual personalities.

may not be the breed for you at all. If, for example, you know you have a particularly unruly child, you really must say so. It may be difficult to admit to, but for the sake of the puppy and long-term harmony in the household, this must be discussed.

Having said that, when you go to visit a litter for the first time, on the assumption that there will also be a second visit, it may be sensible to leave the children at home. If you have a partner, both of you should visit, as the puppy

must be suitable for you both, and the breeder will certainly want to meet you. Children can be very persuasive, so, without them, you will probably be able to make a more considered decision as to whether this is the right litter from which to buy. On the second visit, the children should go along with you so that both you and the breeder can see how they interact.

Do please try to be on time for your appointment, for unless you have had a litter, you will not

know how important timing is. The breeder will be anxious that you see them clean and tidy, and puppies 'pee' and 'poo' a lot. The breeder may even have timed your visit to coincide with mealtime for the puppies, or otherwise perhaps, and puppies' routine cannot be thrown out of sync at this young age. If you are delayed *en route* for some unavoidable reason, please telephone the breeder to explain; I can assure you that this will be much appreciated.

Keep in mind that the dam of the litter may be very protective of her puppies, especially if they are still young, so only approach them if the breeder feels it is right for you to do so. Respect her wishes if she prefers you not to handle them at this early age. She will not want the dam to be upset and, of course, there is always a risk of infection, so never visit a litter if you have been exposed to a possible infection, and make sure your hands and clothes are clean. You may be asked to take off your shoes before entering the home; again, this is understandable with young pups around.

It goes without saying that all the puppies in the litter should look in the best of health, with no runny eyes or tacky bottoms. Their coats will still be quite short, but they should have an abundance of clean hair, and their tummies should be rounded, though not too bulbous, as this may be an indication of worms. Their environment should be scrupulously clean. It may be interesting to note that a good growth of hair on the stomach is an indication that the puppy will become heavily coated in adulthood.

Regardless of whether you are aiming to take home a puppy as a pet or for the show ring, your intention must be that the puppy will remain with you for life. This means it is imperative that you completely fall in love with the puppy, and if you have any reservations at all, then this may not be the Lhasa Apso for you.

SHOW PROSPECT

If you are looking for an Apso as a show dog, you will probably need to be guided by the breeder as to which one has the most potential, but always remember that nothing can be certain. You can never buy 'a show puppy', but you can buy one 'with show potential'. Puppies can change as they grow up, and faults in construction may not show up until later.

A typical problem when selecting an Apso puppy for the show ring is knowing how the dentition will turn out. Breeding lines develop differently, so only the breeder will have any idea whether the bite is more likely to go right, or wrong, in maturity. Many a promising puppy has shattered his owner's dreams when a seemingly good mouth had gone grossly undershot, or has misplaced teeth, or even six lower and upper incisors in the 'first mouth' but fewer when the second set of teeth grow through.

The breeder will help you to assess show potential.

GETTING TO KNOW THE BREEDER

Before visiting the litter of puppies you will doubtless have had a long chat on the phone, with questions fired from both sides. Many good breeders turn away potential puppy buyers at this stage, so if you have been invited to visit, there is an increased chance that the breeder may consider you a suitable owner.

It is also important that you are confident with the breeder. He or she must be someone you feel you can trust and to whom you can turn if you have any questions at all about the health and welfare of your Apso puppy throughout its life. As time progresses you will get to understand your dog's habits and ways, and you will learn to understand if he is perhaps feeling 'off colour'. But the first few days and weeks can be difficult, and you do not want to feel you have no one to turn to.

Lhasa Apsos are temperamentally very different from many of the more 'laid back' breeds, which is all the more reason that you have someone only a telephone call away if you feel you need to chat to ascertain that what your puppy is doing is normal for the breed. You may be having problems with the feeding routine, which is again something you should be able to discuss freely with the breeder.

When meeting the breeder, although you will plan to keep the puppy for the duration of its life, a good breeder will always offer to have the puppy back should the unforeseeable happen. This should be ascertained from the very outset. Personally, when selling a puppy I always give a letter confirming the puppy's identity and stating that I am prepared to take the dog back at any stage of its life. I ask the owner also to sign, agreeing to this arrangement should ever the unfortunate occasion arise.

It is generally accepted that if, on your first visit to view a litter, you decide to purchase a puppy, a deposit is handed over and the balance paid when you go along to collect. Obviously, you must also be sure you understand fully what vaccinations are or are not included in the fee and whether breeding restrictions apply. Some breeders place restrictions on the puppies they sell and these will be detailed in the Kennel Club documentation received. Such restrictions should have been discussed fully beforehand. The most common are that a bitch cannot be bred from and that a male cannot be used at stud, but these restrictions can sometimes be lifted at a later stage with the breeder's consent, when she is confident that the Apso has grown up to be of sufficient quality to procreate.

CHOOSING AN OLDER DOG

Although the benefits of buying a young Lhasa Apso puppy are manyfold, there may be a situation where an owner prefers a slightly older dog, possibly because the demands of a boisterous young puppy are a little too much for them, or perhaps because they would just like to give a good home to an

Sometimes a breeder will run on two puppies before deciding which to exhibit in the show ring.

Apso who has, for whatever reason, 'fallen on hard times'.

There are several reasons why older dogs are occasionally available and you must be as certain as you can be why the dog is being offered for re-sale. You should also bear in mind that if you are looking for a show dog, you are unlikely to find an older dog available for show purposes unless you are willing to pay a very high price. Occasionally, successful winning stock is sold on to a breeder/exhibitor abroad, but the fee paid usually runs into thousands of pounds.

Some breeders like to 'run on' more than one puppy from a litter, with the aim of eventually keeping the better of the two. Sometimes they may even retain three, to keep their options open. Even so, it is unlikely that the puppies who are eventually to leave will be very old when they are offered for sale, perhaps six months or so.

As with any breed, a promising show puppy may simply not turn out well enough for the show ring. This can be especially so in the Lhasa Apso because the mouth formation is not an easy one to breed true to type. A puppy's first set of teeth may look fine, but, when the second set appears, they may be rather too undershot, jumbled, or simply set wrongly in the jaw, which would spoil their chances of winning high honours. It is also possible that a puppy who has a full set of upper and lower incisors in the first mouth

You may decide that an older dog will be better suited to your lifestyle.

develops a tooth or two short when the second set appears. This can be disheartening for any breeder, and, unless the breeder can accommodate a 'passenger' and has an especially soft heart, the youngster may indeed be offered for sale to a pet home. It is possible that the price of a slightly older puppy offered for sale for this reason will be rather less than that of an eight- to 12-week-old youngster.

If purchasing an older puppy as described above, the chances are that he will be at least partly

house-trained However, bear in mind that when a dog goes to a new home he will not know the 'house rules' and will almost certainly need a little re-training. A bonus is that the older dog will hopefully already have been trained to walk on a lead, and the course of vaccinations should be complete.

Another possibility of an older dog coming up for sale is when a breeder decides to part with a bitch that has been used for breeding purposes. It may be that she has suffered an illness at

Some breeders (but by no means all) like to find homes for their bitches once their breeding days are over.

a relatively young age, which has caused her to be spayed and can therefore no longer produce puppies. It may be that she has had a couple or more litters and the breeder now feels it would be best for her to have a different, loving home where she would receive more attention than the breeder is able to offer. It may be that a particular dog or bitch does not get along well with other dogs belonging to the breeder, so they reach a decision to let the 'offender' go so as to return to a state of harmony in the household. This does not necessarily mean that this dog will cause trouble in the future, just that it has decided to 'pick on' one or more of the breeder's other dogs, something that can

easily happen in a pack situation. However, you should only consider such a dog if you have no other pet dogs, just in case!

RESCUED DOGS

Another way of obtaining an older Lhasa Apso, and one that can be highly rewarding, is to take on a rescued dog. A dog can have become 'a rescue' for a whole host of reasons, some of them very valid, such as when an owner has either died or had to be taken into a care home where pets are not allowed. There are other cases that are not so valid, such as when a new baby arrives in the household and the decision is made for the dog to go! This should never be allowed to happen, but sadly it does; this

matter should have been carefully considered before a puppy joined the family in the first instance.

There are also occasions when a dog has a temperament unsuitable for his former home situation. Most good rescue officers will carefully assess a dog's temperament before rehoming and, if necessary, the dog will be kindly put to sleep if it is thought he could not be rehomed safely. There are others, though, that can be suitable for other homes, provided the dog's past history and the potentially new environment are very carefully considered.

FINDING A RESCUED DOG

The best places to locate Lhasa Apsos that are in need of 'rescue

Occasionally, a crossbreed, such as this Apso-Poodle cross may be found in one of the rescue organisations.
© Carol Ann Johnson

homes' are the breed specialist clubs. There are several Lhasa Apso breed clubs in the UK and details of how to contact them can be obtained from the Kennel Club. Most are regional clubs, but the Lhasa Apso Club covers the whole of the country. The best route is for you to get in touch with the club secretary, who can put you in touch with the rescue officer. Very occasionally, a Lhasa Apso, or perhaps a Lhasa Apso crossed with another breed, can also be found in another, larger, rescue organisation.

What you will be asked to pay for a rescued dog depends on several things. You may just be asked to give a donation, or perhaps to cover the cost of any veterinary treatment the dog has had while in the care of the rescue kennels.

People who have had dogs through breed rescue societies are always asked to keep in touch so that a track can be kept of the Apso's progress. In breed clubs' newsletters there are many a heartening stories of Lhasa Apsos that have moved to their new homes, where they have found a

bountiful supply of happiness, despite their unfortunate past histories.

YOUR NEW DOG

A Lhasa Apso is a very special breed and needs rather more care, understanding and grooming than the vast majority of breeds. Hopefully you will have done an enormous amount of research before deciding that this is truly the breed for you – but if you have, you can be assured that you will have wonderful companion for life, a breed I, personally, could never be without!

THE NEW ARRIVAL

4 Chapter

The day you and your family have been building up to has finally arrived! You will have been planning for weeks, probably months, and I hope you will now have everything set and ready to go for the arrival of your new Lhasa Apso. Most probably you will be bringing a puppy home, but it could be an older dog; whichever the case, the excitement will be immense.

You really must start as you mean to go on, and the safety of your Apso must always be uppermost in your mind. When your new dog first arrives at your home he will not know where he is and everything will be unfamiliar to him, so take care that accidents do not happen; it would be simply awful if your puppy met with some unfortunate disaster immediately upon arrival home!

GARDEN SAFETY

Your garden must be ultra-safe, and you must also remember that a Lhasa Apso is only a small dog so can easily locate the tiniest nook or cranny and use this as a means of escape. Pay particular attention to your garden's boundaries. Not all Apsos climb, but some do, so this should also be borne in mind. I once had an Apso that didn't learn to climb until he was 11 years old, but when he did, there was no stopping him!

The garden gate should be very secure and every member of the family should have strict instructions that it should always be firmly closed. To be on the safe side, you may consider erecting a second, small gate, as a means of security. I just have an extra three-foot gate at the side of the house, so that if tradesmen are allowed through the side gate, the dogs cannot rush up to them

– they can just give their warning bark from a safe distance!

If you have an ornamental iron gate, you may well need to change this, or line it with something through which a small Lhasa Apso cannot wriggle, especially when just a puppy. An Apso's coat can make him look deceptively larger than he is, but if you flatten the coat down and measure across the widest point of his ribcage, you will know whether or not you need to make adjustments to your garden. If you have to put up an additional protective covering on your gate, don't use something as fine as chicken wire as your Apso's teeth could get caught in this with disastrous results.

When assessing your garden, you should also consider any places that are unsafe, such as terracing from which your Apso could jump down from a considerable height. Something that may not look particularly dangerous to us as humans would be a mammoth leap for a tiny dog.

SAFETY IN THE HOME

Your home should be a place of comfort and security for your Lhasa Apso puppy, but it can be a place of danger, too. Some hazards for a puppy may be obvious, but there are other hidden dangers, so it is always better to be safe than sorry.

Many things that are dangerous for a dog, especially for a young puppy, are sufficiently high up and therefore out of reach, though you should never forget that Apsos can climb and an inquisitive nose will often go to any lengths to reach an enticing smell, or indeed anything that might capture a dog's interest.

Most people know that chocolate is dangerous for dogs to eat, so we would never knowingly feed it to our dogs or allow them to steal it, but I was caught out on one occasion when I had left a glass of sweet sherry and a box of After Eight mints on a coffee table in the sitting room. I was only away for a moment or two, but when I returned, I found one of my Apsos with her back legs on the sofa and front legs on the coffee table. She had

Security must be uppermost in your mind as the Lhasa Apso can be a great escape artist.
© *Carol Ann Johnson*

already downed the sherry, which had been a full glass, and was merrily munching her way through the After Eights. The uncompromising position in which she found herself made immediate withdrawal impossible for her, so she was truly caught in the act! Fortunately, she suffered no ill effects – but she taught me that an Apso can get up to mischief in seconds!

Because an Apso is fairly low to the ground, this breed is often able to squeeze into places that larger dogs cannot reach. Therefore, check everything at floor level that is easily accessible. However laborious the task may be, you need to check every room in the house, and if it

means going down on all fours yourself, so be it!

The most obviously dangerous items are electric cables, many of which are usually secreted at floor level, behind the TV, computer system and such like. Many a puppy has secretly nibbled away slowly at the casings around wires, sometimes for days, until eventually the electric cable is reached and the consequences can be fatal.

Obviously, all chemicals should be kept out of a puppy's reach, as should household cleaning items; many contain ingredients that can be very harmful if eaten, or sometimes only if touched with the tongue. Pesticides are a real threat, especially slug, mouse and rat poisons, which can cause serious harm, often not noticed until bleeding occurs, possibly from the dog's gums. If ever your Apso puppy or adult dog appears to have been taken ill due to poisoning, it will help your vet enormously if, when you rush your dog to the vet's, you also take along the box or bottle you believe to have caused the illness, as different poisons often have to be treated in different ways. Quick thinking on your part could save your Apso's life.

Remember, too, that many foods you generally keep in your

TOILETING AREA

When your Apso arrives, he will have no idea where he is expected to do his toilet, so you will need to teach him what is required. If you have young children, it is a sensible idea to cordon off an area of your garden that your puppy can be trained to use by simply leading him to this every time he goes outside for this purpose. Soon enough he will become accustomed to this area and will, hopefully, use it regularly of his own accord when he grows up.

All faeces must be picked up and disposed of as quickly as possible, for if it is left lying around, it can become a potential health hazard, and in warmer months of the year will attract flies. If your Apso has been taught to eliminate on a hard surface, rather than on the grass, this will be easier to hose down and keep ultra-clean.

I have never yet had an Apso who eats faeces (copography) but I'm sure there must be a few out there who do have this very unpleasant habit. Keeping their toilet area clean will prevent those that are tempted.

kitchen cupboards can be harmful to dogs. Not only chocolate, but also cocoa powder can be a killer if eaten in large quantities. Raisins and grapes are also especially harmful, so if you drop one or two in error, be sure to pick them up with great speed, before your dog does! Watch nuts, too, especially macadamia.

Parents with children, especially young ones, should teach them that, for the puppy's safety, they must keep all their playthings tidy. Not only can a puppy's teeth cause enormous damage to a much-loved toy, a toy can also harm a puppy, probably causing him to choke. Some children's toys, such as Lego, can be particularly unsafe, as the small pieces are just the

right size to get stuck in a puppy's throat.

Another great danger, not immediately evident, is glue. Very sadly, a puppy I once sold died while still only a few months old, because it had eaten a child's glue used to repair a bicycle wheel. Many children also have games consoles, the wires of which can be very tempting for an Apso puppy.

Stairs are another danger for puppies, as are railings, though which a small puppy might fall. An Apso's coat is abundant, so don't be deceived by the width of the aperture through which he can wriggle or perhaps run through at full pelt while playing. Measure your puppy as described earlier and make sure that your railings are significantly narrower.

If not, you must erect some protection, if only as a temporary measure until he matures.

Apart from the obvious danger of a puppy falling down the stairs and doing himself damage, you should always keep in mind that a Lhasa Apso is a relatively long-bodied dog, so stairs are not so easy for him to negotiate as they might be for other breeds. I have had two Apsos who have been able to get to the top of the stairs, but have never been able to work out how to get down.

A wise precaution is to erect a baby gate, or, better still, a dog gate (usually available from dog shows or from the internet). The gate can be set up at the bottom of the stairs if you wish your Apso to stay only on the ground floor; or indeed you may decide

An inquisitive Apso puppy can get into mischief in no time.

Certainly a new puppy should be crate trained, for there are certainly times when a crate can come in useful; if he were to have to visit the vet's for an operation, he would be crated there, so if he is already familiar with using one, this will make his time in the veterinary surgery far less stressful. If you enter your Lhasa Apso for a Championship dog show, he has to be crated at the show, and it is always safer for a dog to travel in crate for a car journey, rather than to sit on the seat. Should you be involved in a traffic accident, your dog will stand a much better chance of coming off unscathed if he is confined to a crate in the car – and there will be less chance of distracting the driver if a puppy is not jumping around the seats.

Although, when first introduced to a crate, a puppy may not take easily to the idea, if properly trained, he will soon get used to it and come to consider it as his own special place. It is always a good idea to confine a puppy to a crate for very short periods while you are in the house, so you can keep an eye on him. Then, when you need to leave him in a crate for a while for a genuine reason, you will feel secure in your mind that he will be happy if shut in for a while.

Many people who do not have dogs, and indeed many who do, are not at all fond of crates, but crates are not cages, and if you leave the crate door open with a comfortable bed inside, and perhaps a toy, you will often find

to have one at the top and one at the bottom. These are not permanent fixtures and can always be removed once you are confident that your Apso will come to no harm on the stairs. Afterwards these baby or dog gates can come in very handy if fitted across a doorway, to keep your dog in, or out, of the kitchen, for example.

BUYING EQUIPMENT
It is important to ensure that everything is ready for the homecoming to make your puppy's transition from one home to the next as smooth as possible.

CRATE
Personally, although I have crates, my dogs use them rarely, primarily just for travelling and when my dogs are at shows. But their uses are manyfold and quite a lot of owners like their dogs to sleep in crates, which may be understandable, depending on the set-up at home.

IDENTIFICATION

In Britain it is a legal requirement for all dogs to carry a visible form of identification when out in a public place, so even if you have your Apso microchipped, he will still need a tag around his neck, giving contact details should he get lost.

Tags come in two types: those that are engraved, often available from shoe-repair shops, and those on which details are hand-written and contained in a tiny barrel attached to the dog's collar. The latter must be checked on a daily basis to be sure the bottom of the barrel has not come undone and fallen off. Always keep spares in stock. Because of the length of an adult Lhasa Apso's coat, you must also check regularly that hair has not become entangled in the fastening.

In addition to the wearing of a tag attached to the collar, some people have their Apsos microchipped, or have the ears tattooed. For me, I consider the former far preferable for Lhasa Apsos. The microchip that is inserted between the shoulder blades is the size of a grain of rice, but I have only ever had one of my Apsos flinch when it was inserted, and that was only for a fleeting moment. If a dog is travelling abroad, microchipping is essential.

You may wish to consider getting some permanent form of ID for your Lhasa Apso.

CRATE TRAINING

It is an important first lesson for a puppy to learn to settle in a crate.

An Apso that is crate trained makes an easy and adaptable traveller.

that your Apso goes in there of his own free will.

You may decide to have one crate for inside the home and another for travelling with. This will save you the effort of humping it in and out of the car, even though most crates are collapsible. Select your crate/s carefully, though. It must be sufficiently large for your dog to stand up in, and big enough for him to turn around and lie down comfortably. Crates come in varying qualities, and the more expensive ones can last for many a long year, so it is probably better to fork out a little more

money to get the best crate from the start. Check, too, that the safety catch is a good one; this is an area that can be lacking in some of the cheaper models.

Inside the crate you will line the base with newspaper, and then add veterinary bedding, which is easy to wash and must always be kept scrupulously clean. If you have difficulty obtaining this type of bedding at a pet store, you are sure to find it at any of the larger Championship shows. It comes in large sheets, so you can cut it to size and have spare pieces available when one is being

washed. You will also need a water bowl suitable for a crate. I find the best type is the one that hooks on to the side of the crate, but non-spill bowls are also available for travelling. Some owners prefer 'rabbit feeders', but not all dogs take easily to these.

As your Apso reaches maturity and knows all the rules of the house, you may decide to dispense with a crate inside the home and replace this with a typical dog bed, but he must always have a place to call his own. I would, however, urge you still to use a crate when travelling in the car.

FEEDING BOWLS

Stainless-steel feeding bowls are undoubtedly the most hygienic; not only can they be easily washed, but there is no chance of them becoming cracked or chipped and thereby harbouring germs. Stainless-steel bowls are readily available from pet stores and major retail outlets. The second choice would be ceramic bowls; some owners prefer to use these for water, as they are heavier and less likely to spill, but avoid plastic bowls at all costs, as they can be very easily be chewed, particularly by sharp puppy teeth!

COLLAR AND LEAD

When your puppy first comes home he will need a secure collar and lead of suitable size – one that is thoroughly safe, but not too heavy. Be certain that the catch is secure, both on the collar and at the end of the lead. Most collars are adjustable, but be careful not to make the collar so loose that it can slip over the puppy's head if, for example, he decides to pull in the opposite direction. On the other hand, the collar should never be too tight; check that you can slide one or two fingers beneath it.

As your puppy grows, you will need to get a larger collar and more substantial lead. The choice is endless, but if you plan to keep your Apso in long coat, don't select a rolled-leather collar, as the coat will get twisted around it.

There is a wide variety of collars and leads to choose from.

If you plan to show your Lhasa Apso, you will also need one or more show leads; most of us have a bag full, although there is always a favourite. There are various slightly different types of show lead, and you may need to experiment with two or three of these before deciding with suits you best.

GROOMING EQUIPMENT

Because you have chosen a heavily coated breed, grooming equipment will require some investment. While your puppy is still young, you will be able to get away with a high-quality brush, a steel-toothed comb and a pair of nail clippers. Some Apso owners also use a slicker brush, but this must be as soft as possible for a puppy. For adult dogs, the brush should never be of the hardest variety.

Grooming will be an essential part of daily care for your Lhasa Apso, whether he is kept in long coat or in pet trim, so you should already have the basic grooming tools ready and waiting for when you collect your puppy. As soon as he has settled in, perhaps on the second or third day, mini grooming sessions should commence. Hopefully, he will have come to you looking spick and span, but although you may think he does not need to be groomed, you must start to get him used to the routine.

It is also a good idea to get him used to having his teeth cleaned at a young age, so I suggest you invest in some canine toothpaste and a child's toothbrush. A puppy's teeth do not really need cleaning, but you should start as you mean to go on and get him into practice while he's still young.

As your puppy grows older you will need to increase the amount of grooming equipment you have for him, and I know you will feel very proud when his head-fall is long enough to tie up in elastics on each side of his head. I would

Initially your Apso puppy will not need much grooming, but it is important that he gets used to the procedure.

The toys you buy must be 100 per cent safe, and they must be a suitable size for an Apso puppy.

suggest you try to get these bands early, as they are not easily available, other than from shows. The usual elastic bands are far too large; what you will need are 'dental elastics'. Remember not to pull them out or you will break the coat; they should be cut out carefully with scissors each time they are changed. For more information on grooming, see Chapter Five: The Best of Care.

TOYS AND TREATS

Most Apsos like to play with toys, but there are exceptions. Many of mine seem to get more pleasure out of a sock they have surreptitiously dragged out of the bathroom than they do from a whole box full of toys. Others have one special favourite toy, while still others enjoy a wide selection.

When choosing toys for your new Apso puppy, make sure they not too large – but not small enough to swallow. They should not be too heavy or he will not be able to carry them around, nor should they be of the kind to be tugged on. Always remember that a Lhasa Apso's teeth are very different from the norm and you should allow them to develop naturally. Never tug at a toy in an Apso's mouth, especially while he is still a puppy.

Check toys regularly to see that no parts have come loose. If pieces become detached, especially the squeaky parts inside, these can be very dangerous. Toys that start to look dubious in terms of safety should be discreetly removed and thrown away. Bear in mind that if the stuffing becomes detached that, too, can be very dangerous, both for a puppy and for an adult dog.

Chew sticks are enjoyed by puppies, but they that can become sticky when moist and cause havoc with an Apso's coat. Pigs' ears also seem to be very popular, but can get smelly when a dog has been chewing at them for a few days. In all cases, when a chew starts to become small enough to swallow, and certainly if it develops any sharp edges, remove it discretely, but immediately replace with a suitable alternative.

FOOD
Before collecting your puppy, the breeder should give you precise instructions about his current feeding regime. This will enable to you purchase a supply of exactly the same brand of food so that there will be as little disruption as possible to his diet. The diet can be changed over the coming weeks, but this must be done gradually, carefully blending the two and gradually increasing the amount of the new food so as to avoid an upset tummy.

It is not unusual for breeders to provide sufficient food to feed a puppy for a few days after his arrival in his new home, but his should be clarified beforehand so you don't find yourself in the difficult situation of not being able to purchase the right kind of food at short notice. A few breeders are also agents who sell food, in which case you will easily be able to purchase a large bag of food until you find a local supplier.

A change of water can also cause a bit of tummy trouble, especially if your puppy has travelled from a different part of the country where water is different. It is sometimes sensible to use mineral water for the first few days, and to introduce your own tap water slowly. An alternative is to boil the tap water and let it cool before offering it to your dog.

POO BAGS
In Britain, as in many other countries, the law obliges you to clean up after your dog, with strict penalties imposed if you fail to do so. Added to this, there is simply a matter of hygiene and surely none of us wants to further aggravate the anti-dog lobby, which will look for any excuse to complain about dogs and their owners.

Poo bags are inexpensive and can be purchased from many pet stores. A cheaper alternative is to buy nappy bags from a chemist or supermarket. You can even recycle carrier bags, provided they do not have holes in the bottom!

FINDING A VET
If you have bought your Apso from a breeder very close to home, you will probably be able to use the same vet, which, if the vet is a good one, will be an added bonus for there will be continuity. If this is not the case, the breeder may be able to recommend a practice close to you, or put you in touch with someone who can give you first-hand advice.

If your breeder is not in a position to help, make careful enquiries about the vets in your

Most breeders will give you a sample of food so there is no need to change diet in the first few days.

Ideally, you want to find a vet who has experience with Lhasa Apsos.

own area, seeking personal recommendation if possible. In towns and cities, most vets are familiar primarily with small animals, but in a rural practice many have more experience with large farm animals than they do with dogs. It is a 'small animal vet' that you will need, or at least one who deals with both.

Some vets do not understand an Apso's jaw formation, so don't be put off by a vet who tells you that your puppy has an incorrect bite. A reverse scissor bite is correct for the breed, so don't let your vet tell you otherwise.

A few vets incorporate homoeopathy with traditional

veterinary medicine, so if available, this may be a suitable option, though it is a matter for personal preference.

It is always wise to visit a surgery before making your first appointment; this will serve to give you a 'feel' for the place and you can assess its cleanliness and the friendliness of the staff, for you will always want your Apso to be put at ease when visiting. Also check what the surgery times are and whether it is an appointment system or a 'first come first served' basis, which can frequently necessitate a long wait. Check what happens in an emergency outside normal

opening hours. A practice that can respond quickly and efficiently can mean the difference between life and death in a dire emergency. Of course, you hope this will never happen, but it is better to be safe than sorry.

The first occasion you visit your vet will probably be for a routine vaccination, as, depending on your puppy's age upon collection, his course of vaccinations may not be complete. At this time the vet will also check your Apso's general health. The breeder will have provided you with full details of vaccinations to date, including a

SHOPPING LIST

To make sure you are properly prepared for your puppy's arrival, tick off the following items on the list below, at least a couple of days or so before he joins you:

- Crate
- Bed and bedding
- Feeding bowl and water bowl
- Water bowl for travel
- Collar and lead
- Toys and/or treats
- Basic grooming equipment
- Food as advised by the breeder
- Poo bags

After all the hard work of rearing a litter, it is time for the breeder to say goodbye.

record card, and you will need to hand this to your vet so that he knows exactly what drugs have been administered and when.

You should also have been provided with details of the puppy's worming programme, so this, too, should be discussed with your vet so that he can prescribe whatever he considers suitable for continuation, with details of timing. Worming products prescribed by a vet are much more efficient that those available over the counter.

A Lhasa Apso puppy will need to be bathed frequently, so, hopefully, fleas will never be a problem. However, they can be

picked up occasionally from other dogs, even if yours is spotlessly clean, so don't be ashamed of this. 'Spot-on' treatments are available from your vet and last for several weeks. The small amount of liquid is applied behind the dog's neck, to it cannot be licked, and this is absorbed into the skin. It could be wise to purchase a small quantity of this just to keep in your cupboard at home. Do check the expiry date before using. For more information on parasites: see Chapter Eight: Happy and Healthy.

Lastly, if you have decided to have your Lhasa Apso

microchipped, this can also been done by your vet, though I would always prefer not to do this on a puppy's first visit.

COLLECTING YOUR PUPPY

If possible, make arrangements to collect your puppy fairly early in the day, especially if you have a long journey home ahead of you. This will give you as much time as possible with your puppy to help him settle down before bedtime.

Go prepared, armed with plenty of paper towels, damp cloths and dry towels, as quite a lot of Apso puppies do not travel well at first. Most soon get used

PAPERWORK

Although your entire attention is sure to revolve around your new puppy, make sure you are given the important documentation that the breeder should have ready for you. You should be given the Kennel Club registration certificate, a pedigree (ideally five generations), a receipt, a feeding plan, and a list of medications so far administered, including the worming regime that should already have been commenced. The breeder may also have asked you to sign a statement confirming that if ever you are unable to keep the Apso, he will be returned to the breeder. If the breeder has agreed to give you some food for the puppy's next few feeds, remember to take that home with you too.

The breeder may also provide free insurance for the first few weeks of the puppy's time with you. It will then be up to you whether you decide to continue to insure with this provider or change to another company. Of course, you may decide not to take out insurance for the future, but it would be advisable to do so.

to it, but may dribble a lot or even be sick, especially if the car journey takes them on twisty roads. It is also likely that your puppy cannot be put down in public places if his course of vaccinations is not complete, so if his journey is long, you will have to make some provision for an opportunity for him to relieve himself, so carry with you plenty of clean newspaper.

A small water bowl is also essential for the journey, with a bottle of mineral water or boiled tap water that has been left to cool. Your puppy may refuse a drink on the way home, but it must be available, especially in hot weather.

If the breeder is thoughtful, you may be given a small piece of bedding from the whelping box, which will help your little Apso to feel more secure on his journey. In any event you should carry with you something that will be comfortable for him to sit on.

If you are using a crate in the car, rather than putting your puppy alone in the back, place the crate on one of the collapsible seats in the rear and recruit someone to sit on the adjacent seat to give him reassurance and to check he is not being sick. Don't forget to have a drink of water always at the ready, as he may become very thirsty if stressed.

MEETING THE FAMILY

The puppy's arrival at his new home will be overwhelming for him, so initially keep introductions just to the close members of your family. Of course, everyone will want to meet the new youngster that has just joined your life. But the puppy needs to get to know those who will become the closest to him before meeting others, otherwise he will not only become even more overwhelmed, but increasingly confused. He needs to get to know the people who will look after him all the time so that his faith in them can grow and, with it, respect for his new family circle.

Explain to all those people who are anxious to meet your puppy that you want to give him a settling-in period, so that he can develop into a well-adjusted Lhasa Apso adult.

Always keep in mind that this

is the first time your puppy will have left his siblings and also his dam, so he will undoubtedly feel very much 'alone'. You should carry him into the house calmly and without appearing to be over-excited. If there are children at home waiting for the puppy's arrival, you should have instructed them beforehand that they should be waiting as calmly as possible, sitting down, preferably on the floor, rather than running around. A Lhasa Apso puppy is very small, so he is likely to feel intimidated by large human beings towering above him, especially if they are rushing around from place to place.

But before meeting the children, the first port of call will be puppy's toilet area; he may have had a long journey and is probably desperate to relieve himself. Then show him his crate or sleeping quarters, and only then introduce him, calmly, to the children who, as the days and weeks progress, are sure to become an integral part of his life.

Do not allow the children to pick up the puppy at this early stage, at least not the young ones. Just encourage them to stroke him gently, always approaching from under the chin rather than from above the head. After the initial introductions are over, you may well find that your puppy has settled down sufficiently to want to explore his surroundings, but only allow him to investigate those areas in the close vicinity. He will need to

Arriving in a new home is a daunting experience.

become familiar with just one or two areas at a time. If you have a large garden, you should probably wait several days before you allow him the free run of the entire area.

Little by little, over the coming days, you will be able to introduce him to your wider circle of family and friends, and when his course of vaccinations is complete you will be able to introduce him to other dogs. Socialisation at a young age will be an essential part of your puppy's mental development, allowing him to become a well-adjusted companion.

PETS WELCOME
Your puppy will need to be

introduced slowly and carefully to the other pets in your household, always under close supervision. It is unlikely that your puppy will take an aversion to them, but they may decide they are not so fond of him.

If you already have an older dog, it is likely that the puppy will be submissive, and usually the older of the two will realise the puppy is only a youngster and will be gentle with him. But you should always be on your guard and never leave them alone together until you feel certain that their relationship is stable.

It is always wise to introduce dogs on 'neutral' territory. Do not, for example, let the puppy go bounding up to your older

It will not take long for a puppy and an older dog to establish a stable relationship.
© Carol Ann Johnson

dog on his bed, which he will probably guard, and this will not bode well for their future relationship. Never ignore your older dog in favour of the puppy; you should, when possible, greet the older dog first followed by the youngster. In time they will sort out their own pecking order.

Another situation that can cause tension is mealtimes. Never feed both dogs from the same dish, and keep the dishes well apart when meals are served. You need to know exactly what the young puppy is eating – and you don't want his food gulped down without notice by a hungry adult! Likewise, beds should be kept apart, and obviously each dog should have his own base. In time they may happily snuggle up together in the same basket, but they must each have the

opportunity to have their private space when they want it. If your older dog has his own special toy, make sure you have bought another toy for the puppy, as the older dog may just be jealous if the youngster tries to steal his. Again, in time, they will probably share their toys freely, but avoid any unnecessary aggravation from the outset.

Introducing the family cat can be a different matter. I have always found that cats keep their distance from the newcomer for a few days, without either party being restricted, but others feel it best to crate the puppy and let the cat into the room to sniff around, following which the puppy is let out on a lead. In theory the latter may be a good idea, but Apsos don't always take easily to lead training, so it may

be a good few days before the best-laid plans actually work! Just take care that the cat does not lash out at your puppy's eyes.

Introducing an Apso to smaller pets is not usually a problem, as, more often than not, a rabbit, hamster, mouse or pet rat has his own cage. I have found that rabbits who have freedom around house and garden have always got along well with Lhasa Apsos, though with sighthounds it is quite a different matter!

THE FIRST NIGHT

The very last duty you have to your new puppy before settling him down for the night in his new home is to let him out to his toilet area. Even if he doesn't seem to want to relieve himself, give him time and hopefully he will. This will make for a much more comfortable start to the long, lonely hours of darkness.

Because your puppy will be unfamiliar with his surroundings and undoubtedly missing his dam and siblings, you should put something safe into his crate or sleeping quarters so that he can cuddle up, albeit to an inanimate object, such as a cuddly toy.

HOUSE RULES

Just as with a child, when your Lhasa Apso puppy joins your household he will have to learn what is and what is not expected of him. His mealtimes should be set at regular intervals but, depending on his age, these will probably be reduced in number as he matures. He should have been introduced to his toilet area, and although mistakes are sure to happen in the early days, at least the rules will have been set.

If you do not wish your puppy to get on the bed or other furniture, you must make this clear to him from the outset. It is absolutely no good picking him up to sit with you on one occasion, and telling him to get off the sofa on another. You should also bear in mind that an Apso, being a relatively short-legged, long-bodied breed, should not be allowed to jump up and down from heights that, in relation to his size, are enormous. This can cause him great damage and affect his growing bone structure.

Consistency is of great importance, for if your puppy is allowed to do something on one occasion, and not the next, he

will be a very confused little individual.

House rules do not only apply to your new puppy, but to your family as well. Small children must be taught never to tug at the coat, which, as it grows, may be very tempting. Do not allow children to feed titbits to your puppy; what seems like a very tasty treat to your child may be totally unsuitable for a dog.

Another highly important house rule is that doors and gates should be closed at all times; there would be nothing worse than your precious new friend escaping, and just think how badly the offender would feel, too!

HOUSE TRAINING

A puppy needs to pee and poo much more often than an adult dog, and when he wakes up, he simply can't wait! If he is not already awake, the chances are that when he hears the household stir, he will be up on his feet and ready for the day ahead, so don't wait to get dressed or put the kettle on, let him out straight away before he has time to have an accident.

A puppy will need to relieve himself very often, usually about every one or two hours, and especially after eating and sleeping. This frequency will reduce substantially as he grows up, but, until then, you will need

Take your puppy out at regular intervals so that he learns to be clean in the house.

A puppy will get as much exercise as he needs playing in the garden.

to be vigilant and watch for every sign. Until he knows that he must ask at the door, the first sign will be sniffing the ground, and then probably turning around in a circle, at which time you must pick him up immediately and take him to his toilet area or, when he is a little older, open the door quickly and indicate that he must go out.

Never chastise your puppy unless you actually catch him in the act of doing his toilet in the wrong place. If you do, you will only serve to confuse him, for he will not connect the two and will have absolutely no idea why he is being told off. Most Apsos like to be clean indoors, so house training is not likely to be a

problem, though there is sure to be the occasional accident to start with.

PUPPY EXERCISE

You will need to wait until your puppy's course of vaccinations is complete before you can take him out in public places, but there is no reason why you cannot begin some training in your garden sooner than this. Although some Lhasa Apsos take to a lead fairly readily, many others do not, so the sooner you can start to give him a little practice the better.

Get him used to his collar first of all. This can be attached inside the house and you should always stay with him until he is

comfortable with it, for he is almost certain to try to scratch it off. Although his hair is not yet long, it can still get tangled if he scratches.

Training on the lead should be done in a separate area of your garden away from the toilet area. At first I like my Apso puppy to lead me, so that he basically just gets used to the fact that something is attached to his collar, with which he should already be familiar. Then I gently exert pressure on the lead and soon reach the stage when I can lead him about and call him to me, at first stooping down and enticing him, with or without a titbit.

You will need to wait until your puppy is at least six months old before he is allowed to free run off the lead, and even then only in a very safe place and under close supervision. For more information on training, see Chapter Six.

TAKING ON AN OLDER DOG

In just the same way as a puppy, an older dog may feel very apprehensive when being introduced to his new home; everything will be just as strange for him. His past circumstances will also have a bearing on how easily he can adjust. He may have had an unhappy life, so he may be frightened of things such as doors closing on him, or he may be afraid of people's legs if he has been kicked. Yes, sadly it does happen!

On the other hand, he may

have already enjoyed many happy years living with a devoted owner who has either died or been taken into a care home where dogs are not allowed. In such circumstances he is sure to be missing his owner dreadfully, and you will have to take this into consideration. Indeed, it often takes longer for an older dog to settle into a new home than it does a puppy.

Introduce the older dog to your home much as you would a puppy, and remember that he doesn't know the house rules either. He may have been perfectly clean around the house in his former home, but in your home he is not so sure where he should do his business. For example, if he is used to grass, and you have none, he may decide that your rug is the nearest thing to the texture of grass!

The same rules apply as for a youngster: do not introduce him to all and sundry in one fell swoop. Introduce your family and friends slowly, allowing him to get used to each one individually. Never force yourself on a Lhasa Apso – and do not allow your friends to impose themselves. In his own good time your new pet will strike up his bond of friendship, but it is he who will decide when this will happen, not you, nor your friends and relations. Be patient!

FEEDING

Depending on how you came into contact with your new adult friend, you may have been given a diet sheet by the rescue centre or breed rescue representative from whom you collected your dog. It is unlikely that you will actually have collected the dog from his previous owner, but if this is the case, be sure to ask what food has been given and whether meals have been provided once or twice a day.

As for a puppy, change to the diet should be made slowly so as not to upset your Lhasa Apso's tummy. Don't worry if he is not over-enthusiastic about food for the first couple of days. He will eat when he is hungry, and probably when you are not looking. I have found that many Apsos prefer to eat alone, and some of them like to take a few small pieces away from their dish to eat in a quiet corner somewhere. If your newly acquired pet has not eaten for two full days after arrival, you should consult your vet, but usually an Apso can be enticed with a piece of boneless white chicken meat, and once he has started to eat, hopefully he will never look back. Again, it may be sensible to offer only bottled water or cooled boiled water for the first few days, then gradually introduce your local tap water.

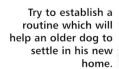

Try to establish a routine which will help an older dog to settle in his new home.

Adopt a calm, no nonsense attitude if your Apso seems worried by new situations.

TRAINING STRATEGY

Although the older Lhasa Apso you have taken on may already be well trained, or reasonably so, you should be prepared for all eventualities so that unsociable situations do not arise.

Because he does not know where he is at first, he may be tempted to bark if left alone outside, so initially you should stay with him to give reassurance. The people who visit your home and even walk past you gate will be different from the people he came across before, so once again reassure him that he has nothing to fear. Don't forget to praise him when he has done something of which you approve.

If he appears overly nervous about something, don't cuddle and cosset him too much or he will pick up on your own vibrations and feel even more unsure. Instead try to ignore him, all the while keeping an eye on him. Then, when he is calm, give him plenty of praise for having been so confident and overcoming his fears.

If house training your new adult Lhasa Apso is a problem at first, don't get angry with him. Soon enough he will learn what he should do, where and when. Apsos like to be clean and he will be as happy as you are when his toileting routine is finally sorted out.

EXERCISE

A newly acquired older Lhasa Apso should be treated in much the same way as a youngster, in that you should introduce him slowly to new situations and walks in different areas. The busiest areas should always be left until last.

Until you are absolutely certain that your Apso is confident with you and has accepted you as his new owner, he should not be let off the lead. Until then, there is always a chance that he will run off and try to find his way back to his original home, for he will have no idea of how far away from his first home he has moved.

LIVING WITH CHILDREN

Whether or not your Apso puppy, or indeed your Lhasa Apso adult, gets along easily with children will depend very largely upon whether he has been raised in a family with children. To a small child, a Lhasa Apso can look very much like a toy – but this is exactly what he is not!

An Apso's coat is always a temptation for a child, but tugging at a coat hurts and, apart from the obvious damage to the coat itself, the pain it causes could result in the dog snapping at the child. This would be the case for any breed, not just the Lhasa Apso. It is therefore imperative that children are introduced to dogs very carefully and are taught exactly what, and what is not, within the realms of possibility when fondling a new pet.

Children should never be left alone with a Lhasa Apso, at least not until you are absolutely confident that they get along well together and that no harm is

Do not allow your Apso off lead until you are confident that he will come back to you.

likely to come to either party.

After a few weeks it may be possible for an older, sensible child to take your dog out for a walk in a secure place. This should not be allowed until everyone is absolutely confident that the dog is happy to walk on a lead and will not be fazed by any situation that

is thrown at him.

If you have obtained your older Lhasa Apso from a rescue society, there should always be someone who is ready to speak to you on the telephone, at least to help you thorough the first few weeks that are so important in establishing a good relationship for the future.

THE BEST OF CARE

5 Chapter

You have chosen to have a Lhasa Apso join your life, so you will want to be certain that you give him the very best of care for the many happy years you will share together. To keep him in good bodily health he must be fed and exercised well, but he will also need mental stimulation and plenty of attention paid to his coat. Grooming is especially important in this breed, whether you keep your Apso in full-length show coat or in a pet trim.

DIET AND NUTRITION
What you feed your Apso will play a very important part in his ultimate health and well-being as well as in the quality and density of his coat. As your puppy has matured into adulthood, you will slowly have adjusted his diet and the feeding routine will fit in with your own lifestyle. Some people

feed only one meal each day, usually in the late afternoon or early evening – never late in the day or he won't have the chance to fully digest it before settling down for the night. If only one main meal is given each day, there should ideally be a small snack at the other end of the day. Other people like to feed two smaller meals each day, but in both cases the overall intake of food should be about the same; two meals a day does not mean two large ones! The Lhasa Apso is not a breed that is particularly prone to excessive weight gain, but bitches who have been spayed need to have a careful eye kept on their diet.

There are many options as to what you actually feed your dog, increasingly so with the enormous variety of ready prepared foods available in the shops, not only in pet stores but in supermarkets, too. The choice is endless.

Although dogs are basically carnivores, they actually benefit from eating plant materials too, so essentially they are omnivorous. All of my Lhasa Apsos have enjoyed vegetables, especially carrots, but personally I would not choose to feed a completely vegetarian diet to any dog, whatever my own preferences.

It is very important to note that all Tibetan dog breeds, and that of course includes the Lhasa Apso, can be intolerant to dairy products, some more than others. If your Lhasa Apso develops a red or pink rash on his tummy, the first thing to consider is whether he may have eaten too much cheese or too many eggs, or whether he has been drinking cows' milk. Goats' milk suits a Lhasa Apso much better than cows' milk, but when they are fully grown most Apsos are perfectly happy with water, though I always like to add a

LIFE-STAGE FEEDING

While your Lhasa Apso is growing he will have a greater need for energy, protein, vitamins and minerals than does a fully-grown adult dog. Bear in mind that a puppy's birth weight roughly doubles in the first seven to 10 days and this will give you an idea of how important it is to feed the correct nutrients.

A puppy needs meals more frequently than an adult, and when an Apso is getting into his teens, he will benefit from more frequent, smaller meals.

little live yoghurt to their diet, at least on an occasional basis.

Cheese and eggs do not need to be totally avoided – all of mine enjoy this food as a special treat – but really only a tiny taste as opposed to a plateful! An exception to this is that when a bitch has whelped, I feed her a raw egg mixed with liquid calcium daily, until her puppies are weaned.

NUTRIENTS IN THE DIET

There are many different nutrients in a dog's diet, and water is important to transport them around the body. If feeding dried food, an Apso will need to drink considerably more water than if he is eating fresh food, roughly two to three parts of water for each part of dried food.

Proteins provide energy and are essential for growth and the repair of body tissue, while carbohydrates are also used to provide energy. It is from fats and oils that energy is supplied in its most concentrated form, and they can also help the absorption of some vitamins.

Only small quantities of vitamins and minerals are needed, but they are essential for many different reasons. Calcium and phosphorous are two prime examples for they are utilised in the make-up of both teeth and bones.

CHOOSING A DIET

PREPARED FOOD
When feeding a diet prepared by a manufacturer, be very careful

The aim is to feed a well balanced diet that is suited to your Lhasa Apso's age and lifestyle.

CHOOSING A DIET

A prepared diet may take the form of canned meat and biscuit (left) or a complete, dry diet (right).

If you are feeding a fresh, homemade diet, you will need to make sure it has all the nutrients your dog requires.

not to unbalance an otherwise well-balanced diet. Humans would not wish to eat the same food day in and day out, but dogs do not think along the same lines, just so long as they feel well fed and well nourished.

Although I feed high-quality dried food myself, I do add just a little 'something' for variety's sake each day; this may be a very small portion of fresh meat or tinned food or even a few fresh vegetables. However, I regularly check my dogs' weight and I know them well enough to notice if any change in diet has caused them to become a fraction more hyperactive than usual or if they have loose motions, something a change in diet can easily cause. Live yoghurt or fresh curd is particularly useful to correct any tummy upsets and loose bowel movements.

HOMEMADE DIET
With today's hectic lifestyle, most owners find it much easier and more convenient to feed a ready prepared food that can be purchased over the counter, but there are people who still like to feed a freshly prepared diet. This is certainly possible, but it is less likely that the diet will be so accurately balanced as a complete canine diet that has been scientifically prepared by a good manufacturer. I stress the word 'good', for the quality of pre-prepared foods can vary considerably, just as they vary greatly in cost.

Many different foods can be used in a canine meal prepared by a dog's owner: fruit vegetables, eggs, rice and, of course, both red and white meats. However, if feeding such a diet, it is usually wise also to give your dog vitamin and mineral

supplements, which are not generally needed otherwise.

BARF DIET
Some owners successfully feed the BARF diet, the name of which stands for Bones And Raw Food, or some say Biologically Appropriate Raw Food. Basically, it just means that dogs are fed the way that nature intended. In the wild, dogs lived off whole carcasses, which included not only the meat, skin and internal organs, but also the contents of the stomach, which usually contained digested vegetation, incorporating essential nutrients.

A BARF diet is essentially a raw diet that is as varied as possible, including lots of raw meaty bones, such as chicken wings, chicken necks, rabbit, oxtail, minced meats, lamb shanks, eggs and their shells, liver, heart, fish, yoghurt, pulped vegetables, and

It is your responsibility to ensure your Lhasa Apso maintains the correct weight.

HEALTH WARNING

Foods that can be harmful to dogs include human chocolate (all colours), including cooking chocolate and cocoa, grapes and raisins, cooked chicken bones and other cooked bones, especially lamb.

fruit. Garlic is also included in the diet, but not all agree with this.

There are those who do not advocate the BARF diet, but there are many who do and I can honestly say that I have come across several Lhasa Apso dog breeders who absolutely swear by it, so this may well be something to consider when coming to a decision about what diet to feed. Personally, I feel that the BARF diet is better suited to smaller dogs than to large ones. I have always found that sighthounds swallow raw foods down dangerously quickly, whereas an Apso enjoys a thorough chew on a raw chicken wing, which pays dividends in the tooth-cleaning department too!

DRINKING WATER

Whatever diet you choose to feed your Lhasa Apso, you must be certain that he always has access to plenty of fresh drinking water. Although always important, this is especially so if you are feeding a diet of dried food. Take care that your dog's bowl never runs dry, as he may well decide to have an enormous drink after a meal, thus leaving his bowl empty without it being noticed.

If you are trying to grow or preserve your Apso's long head furnishings, you can always put them in bands at the side of the head, as well as on the top, if you wish to protect them while eating and drinking.

GUARDING AGAINST OBESITY

The Lhasa Apso is not a breed that easily puts on excess weight but there are some whose weight gain one has to watch. Sentimentality is a frequent reason why dogs are allowed to become overweight. There are times when table scraps can be fed to dogs, possibly as a little treat, but they should never be fed to excess. Scraps that are given must be suitable for a dog to eat and, of course, small cooked bones should never be given. Obviously, sufficient exercise is another very important factor in weight control.

There are severe health implications for a dog carrying

excess weight. These include heart and respiratory problems, and also diabetes.

DIET FOR THE INFIRM OR ELDERLY

Dogs that are unwell will most probably need some alteration to their diet, and your vet can advise on this. Following an operation it is normal to keep a dog on freshly cooked chicken or fish for a couple of days, probably with a little well-cooked brown rice, which is highly nourishing. As the dog recovers from his operation, his normal food can gradually be re-introduced.

Kidney and heart failure are common in older dogs and it is generally accepted that it is prudent to avoid feeding the adult dog too much protein, sodium (salt) and phosphorous in an endeavour to avoid such problems. Over-feeding of these nutrients can be detrimental to dogs, even before there is any evidence of disease.

Older dogs tend to be best fed on smaller meals, so they may have two or even three smallish meals spread throughout the day. As they become less active with old age, protein content can usually be reduced. But if you have any doubts at all about what is right for your dog, seek advice from your vet or from a canine nutritionist.

PET GROOMING

The Lhasa Apso is a high-maintenance breed regarding coat care, even to keep purely as a pet rather than as a show dog. There

Bathing needs to be done on a regular basis. © *Juliette Cunliffe*

are different options that can be adopted for your pet, but whichever direction you choose to take, daily grooming attention will always still be needed.

Some pet owners prefer to keep their Apsos in full coat, but unfortunately this will give your pet some limitations in terms of exercise. For example, if the weather is wet, drying your pet will require time and effort, and there is a high risk of matting. Try to get into the routine of brushing daily with a pin brush and then follow with a wide-tooth comb. A grooming spray can be an asset, making it easier to brush through a dry coat. If you decide to keep your pet Apso in full coat, it is best to keep the underneath short and to keep the feet and pads on the foot trimmed.

If you are going to groom your Apso in full coat yourself, it is wise to invest in some grooming equipment such as a small

grooming table and a lightweight stand dryer. These will make it much easier to groom your pet and wiil free up both of your hands for drying and brushing out at the same time. This method also makes the dog much more accepting of the proceedure. Such items can readily be bought from a supplier that can easily be found via the internet. Investing in some professional equipment will certainly make life easier for you and your Lhasa Apso.

BATHING

You will need to bath once a fortnight, making sure that you have kept the coat tangle-free with daily grooming. If you bath with mats in the coat, these will be hard to get out once dry. The mat tends to tighten up, making it uncomfortable for your pet when you try to tease it out.

You will be able to buy a good conditioning dog shampoo and conditioner from a pet store. It is best not to use human products, as they can be unbalanced with their PH level and can irritate a dog's skin.

Begin by wetting the dog thoroughly, leaving the head till last (this prevents shaking). Apply the shampoo. It is best to dilute with warm water in a large bottle with a squeezy top; something like a washing-up liquid bottle is ideal. Work the shampoo well into the whole body, paying particular attention to the under carriage, bottom area and between the toes. Pay careful attention to avoid getting shampoo in the eyes and inside the ears.

Rinse the shampoo off thoroughly so the coat is squeaky clean. Rinsing is very important; if shampoo is left on the skin, it can cause irritation and itching. Apply the conditioner, as this will make it easier to brush the coat while you dry with the hairdryer. It is best to squeeze the excess water from the coat, being careful not to rub the coat with a towel, as this can cause the coat to tangle. Dry the coat by directing the dryer at the area of coat you are brushing. It is handy to have a spare pair of hands to help you, or invest in a hand-dryer holder that can be attached to the side of a table.

HAIR TIES

Once the coat is totally dry, go through it with a comb and decide how you want to control the hair on the head so that it isn't in your Apso's eyes all the time. You could trim a fringe into the head furnishing or you could tie the hair back into two braids either side of the skull above the eyes. Make sure that the hair that is tied back is not too tight and pulling the skin or eye area.

PROFESSIONAL HELP

A good option is to have your Apso groomed by a professional dog groomer who will be able to style your pet's coat so that it looks attractive yet practical for an unrestricted lifestyle. A visit every three months should be sufficient for routine trimming, which will make life easier for both you and your pet.

You can choose to have a consultation with a professional

You may consider enlisting the help of a professional groomer.
© *Juliette Cunliffe*

groomer so you can describe the type of life that your pet is going to lead. This will enable the groomer to give you advice on different trims. It is also wise to weigh up the cost of the different styles and decide which option suits your budget.

Professional grooming treatment consists of bathing and grooming your pet into the preferred style and clipping the nails. The groomer will also pluck the hair from the ear canal, which must be done so the ear can be kept clear. You will need to keep a check on this between grooms. The anal glands will need to be cleared before the bath. This task should only be carried out by someone who is experienced, as it involves placing external pressure on either side of the anus. If done incorrectly, it can cause an abscess.

The 'puppy' or 'teddy' trim consists of the coat being clipped

short on the back and an amount of hair left on the legs, which is then scissored to give a trouser effect. The head is trimmed so that the eyes are visible. The moustache is scissored quite short, usually level with the ears so that the coat does not interfere with the dog eating or enjoying chew treats.

This type of trim needs to be done by a professional groomer at six- to eight-week intervals. In terms of routine care, the coat will need to be brushed daily with a soft slicker brush, and then combed through to prevent knots occurring in the coat.

Another option is to have the dog clipped with a medium-length blade all over the body and legs. The hair on the head and ears is then scissored short. This type of trim is the best choice for low maintenance and only needs to be done every 12-16 weeks.

ROUTINE CARE

Every morning you need to check your Apso's eyes for sleep or debris. If necessary, wipe it away with a damp cotton pad and then dry the area with a face towel or similar. You also need to make sure your pet's bottom is clean and does not get stuck with faeces; hair will continue to grow around the anus and it is possible when the Apso goes to the toilet that it will get caught in the coat. If you do not feel confident to trim the bottom, speak to your groomer to see if it would be possible for your Apso to have a bath and bottom trim in between his usual grooming sessions.

TEDDY TRIM

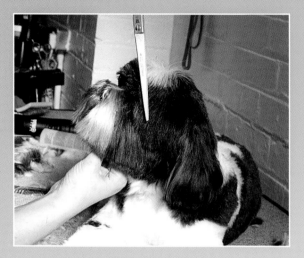

The head is trimmed so the eyes are visible.

The hair on the legs is trimmed to give a trouser effect.

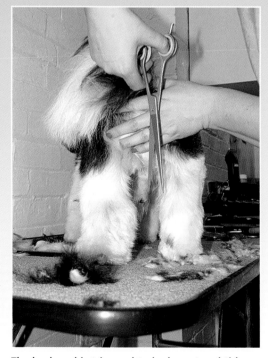

The back end is trimmed to look neat and tidy.

The final result: An Apso in 'puppy' or 'teddy' trim.

ROUTINE CARE

The ears must be checked to ensure they are clean and free from odour. The groomer will also pluck excess hairs from the ear canal.

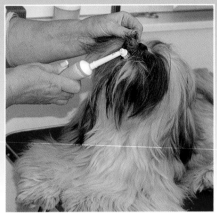

Accustom your Apso to teeth cleaning from an early age.

Your Apso needs to get used to having his teeth cleaned from an early age. There are many teeth-cleaning products on the market, but good-quality canine toothpaste applied with a toothbrush is effective if cleaning is carried out on a daily basis. Check your Apso's mouth for redness on the gums and the build-up of plaque, which can be seen as a brown deposit starting at the top of the tooth next to the gum. A sure sign of a problem with your pet's oral hygiene is an unpleasant smell coming from the mouth or from the nasal passage when the mouth is closed. If you spot any problems, ask the vet for advice. Dental treatment under anaesthetic may be the only option. This may seem drastic – and, unfortunately, can be expensive – but it may well be essential. If oral problems are ignored, they can have a very detrimental long-term effect on

your dog's wellbeing.

It is very important to make grooming a regular routine, as it becomes a very good bonding exercise for you and your pet. The aim is to make grooming sessions pleasurable for your Apso. Grooming will only become uncomfortable for your pet if it is not done regularly. When the coat is allowed to get matted, grooming is an unpleasant experience for the dog, and this is just not fair. If your Lhasa Apso does get matted, the kindest option is to seek professional help to clip the coat down with electric clippers and start again. The coat will grow again very quickly and this is far better than battling with your Apso and making him resent being groomed.

Keeping a Lhasa Apso in good order is certainly hard work, but seeing a well-trimmed and groomed pet Lhasa Apso striding

along with his jaunty gait, is a joy to behold.

SHOW GROOMING

If you make the decision to show your Lhasa Apso, the word 'commitment' is a term that will become a big part of your life. Preparing your Apso and keeping the coat in good condition to achieve the ultimate finished appearance takes dedication and discipline. It is very important that your potential show dog gets plenty of free exercise so that his body condition can reach full potential and, along with a good diet, there is no reason why a glorious finished coat cannot be realised.

Weather permitting, I exercise my dogs daily, so they need to be washed weekly. I always wash them every five to seven days depending on the time of year, and I do not 'dry' groom in between, as I find that this is when coat damage can be caused. Obviously, I always make sure that there is not a build-up of twigs or leaves from their daily exercise.

BATHING

It is very important to find a shampoo and conditioning system that works well for your Apso's type of coat and also that agrees with your pocket. Many of these shampoos are concentrated and it is very important to follow the dilution instructions carefully to achieve optimum results and get the full benefit financially. Some coats do require a richer bathing regime; with some colours the coat does feel harder and is likely to dry out more easily. The particolours, especially grey and whites, tend to be naturally harder in texture, and although this is what the Breed Standard asks for, to achieve a lustrous full coat they require a richer shampoo and conditioning system to keep the moisture levels in the hair shaft. However, all colours can be of this texture and you should seek the advice of a professional groomer or a fellow exhibitor if you are in doubt about the texture of your Apso's coat. Coats that have a slightly softer feel will benefit from a texturising shampoo and conditioner, as it is important to strive to have the hard coat texture that our Breed Standard asks for. I usually find it is best to shampoo twice, making sure that the undercarriage of the dog is especially clean.

If you are showing your Apso, you will need to devote long hours to preparing your dog for competition. © Carol Ann Johnson

The face is an area that needs special attention; it is easy not to clean the face as well as the rest of the body, as there is a worry of shampoo getting in the eyes. It is wise to use a tearless shampoo and one that is hypoallergenic, as this will be free of any perfume and colour and be gentle, yet deep cleaning.

Staining caused by urine on the back legs and on the undercarriage can benefit from shampoos on the market that are usually blue in colour, designed to neutralise the yellow tones. I find that they can be very effective if you apply the shampoo to a dry coat in the affected areas and leave it for a few minutes before starting to wash. In these areas I always use a stronger concentration of my conditioner, as this hair will be more porous (due to the acid in the urine making it weaker), and so it will need more moisture.

Once the coat has been shampooed, I towel off the excess water and then I apply conditioner. Place the conditioner down the coat, starting about two inches (5 cms) from the dog's skin, concentrating on the last third of the hair, as this is the oldest part of the coat and usually the most stressed. If it is possible to apply heat to the coat at this point, it can improve the result. Try to leave the conditioner on the coat for between three to five minutes, making sure the dog is comfortable and that there is no risk of him catching a chill.

DRYING THE COAT

Once rinsed thoroughly, it is time to fluff-dry the coat. A stand dryer is a great investment, as is a good-sized table so that the dog is easily manoeuvred. Try to train your Apso from puppyhood to accept lying on his side for grooming; it makes it easier to brush out the inside of the legs and on the belly.

I find that using a good-quality slicker brush is ideal for drying the coat. Start by brushing the legs when the dog is on his side so that they will have a full appearance. If there is a matted area on the dog, it is best to try to hold the top of the mat where it is closest to the skin and gradually brush the mat through from the base of the area. If you take the pressure of the detangling between your fingers, it stops the skin from being pulled, which is what causes discomfort. Always take great care when brushing mats from the coat and always think of the way it would feel if you were removing a knot from your own hair!

Once one part is dry, go through with a comb to make sure that the coat is tangle-free and no dead coat is left in. I tend to dry from the tail back to the head once the legs are done, to make sure that the area around the kidneys are not damp for very long.

SHOW PRESENTATION

When the coat is totally dry and combed through, I stand the dog and go through the coat with a pin brush, making the parting down the back and thereby setting the shape of the coat. I usually polish the coat with a bristle mix-nylon brush to condition the hair shaft. At this point I will use a light grooming spray based on the conditioning system that has been used for bathing.

Evaluating the coat at this stage is wise to see where improvement needs to be made. It is important to look at the balance of your dog; a dog's balance can be thrown by too much coat on the back end, in the same way that too much on the front half of the dog can make

The standard of presentation is very high at the top level.
© *Carol Ann Johnson*

the dog look top heavy. It is very important, especially in light of the new preface to all the Kennel Club Breed Standards stating that no breed characteristic should be excessive, that the Lhasa Apso's head fall appears balanced. The head fall is important to protect the eyes from the harsh conditions of its native terrain. The correct head shape, plus the length of the Apso's eyelashes, means that he should have no problem seeing through the head fall.

A good way to trim head fall is to use double-thinning shears, twist the coat at the bottom of the head fall, and trim the coat very gradually on a declined angle. Any trimming that needs to be done should be carried out well in advance of shows that you intend to compete in. I tend to trim two to three weeks

beforehand, which gives the coat a chance to settle. Remember: in this case, less is definitely more.

If I am only doing my weekly grooming, I will plait the head coat and tie the moustache hair loosely in a band so that is does not bother the dog when eating or having a chew treat. I do band the back coat away so that, hopefully, any dirty trouser incidents can be avoided.

I avoid grooming sprays that contain alcohol, as they are very drying to the coat. I also steer clear of products that have silicone in them: although these can achieve an illusion, they can be very detrimental to the coat over time. Conditioning creams can have great results and can be very beneficial to conditioning a show coat in-between shows. It is important to remember that due to Kennel Club regulations regarding show preparation, the coat can only be prepared with water as a grooming spray. This is why it is so important to keep a show coat in excellent condition.

It is normal for a puppy to have a wonderful puppy coat and then, when he becomes an adolescent, he 'blows' coat and loses condition as the new adult coat grows through. It is important to remember that the Apso has a double coat and that it is there for a reason: to enable it to adapt to its native Tibetan terrain.

The mature Lhasa Apso in full coat is a spectacular sight, but it does take time and patience. I find that the mature coat really begins to bloom from about the age of four years; the coat texture and coat growth then becomes constant. It is also important to make sure that your show dog is in wonderful muscular condition, and in a good frame of mind, so that the well-presented coat is simply the icing on the cake.

EXERCISE

If you keep more than one Apso in your home, they will get lots of exercise by running around and playing together. If you watch carefully, you will see that they utilise every muscle in their bodies with their various twists and turns. It's all great fun! But if you have only one, although some exercise will naturally be taken around your home and in your garden, you will need to take him on at least one daily walk when an adult.

The British climate is not always conducive to keeping a fully coated Lhasa Apso in good coat when it comes to taking walks in various terrains, but if you have taken on a rescued dog,

A game of retrieve is an excellent way of exercising your Apso.

it is likely that he will already be clipped in 'pet trim', which makes this a lot easier. Raincoats are also available with legs in them, and even little boots can be purchased, but boots are never easy to keep on a dog and you may well find that you only have two or, if you are lucky, three, by the time you arrive home!

Whether or not you allow your Apso off the lead is very much dependent upon how well trained he is, and the safety of the environment in which you are exercising him. His temperament will also play a part in where you take him for his walks and how much freedom you allow him. A prime example is that a dog who has had no exposure to children, and is therefore a little fearful of them,

should not be suddenly taken to the children's playground in your nearby park. Although you may slowly build up to this, he should certainly not have children forced upon him all of a sudden.

Probably because I have lived in the countryside for most of my life with Apsos, I find my own have little or no traffic sense, so this is something you will need to take into account. I have also found that one of mine chased bicycles. He never caught them, but his enthusiasm to pursue them could easily have caused a tragic accident had this happened in the wrong place at the wrong time.

Basically, it all comes down to common sense and to sensible training. If you approach roadwork carefully, taking things one step at a time, your Lhasa Apso should be able to accompany you almost anywhere and enjoy the outing.

CARING FOR THE OLDER DOG

Because an Apso is a long-lived breed, he could be well into double figures before you even realise he is growing old. His teeth may show signs of age, he may be getting thinner, although he seems to eat the same amount, and maybe he won't be so active as he was in his younger days. I have always found that my Apsos have kept their hearing, right until the very end, but I have a few whose sight has dimmed, but only in those who have developed 'dry eye' (keratoconjunctivitis), which I have found tends not to affect them until 12 years or later.

If you are a genuine dog lover, you will wish to give your Lhasa Apso every comfort he deserves in his closing years. He will need adequate warmth, high-quality food and sensible exercise. He will very probably be happier with two or three small meals each day instead of one large one, if that is what you have normally fed. Personally, I have not found that my elderly Apsos have needed a special diet, but there are some who do. There are various 'veteran diets' available, and some are prescription diets obtainable from your vet, but the price of these is by no means cheap.

If some of your Apso's teeth have loosened, fallen out or been removed, you will need to alter the consistency of his food, but never deprive him of his much-loved chewy things, even if he only wants to suck on them now. If feeding a dried food, it may be sensible to soak it in water for about an hour before feeding time, making it easier to swallow and

The needs of your Apso may change as he gets older.
© Carol Ann Johnson

digest. Another alternative would be to feed a puppy meal instead of an adult diet, although you will have to check that the protein level is not too high.

Many old dogs tend to put on weight with age, but this is not something I have found with Apsos; all mine have tended to lose weight, but only in the last year of their lives. If your elderly Apso does seem to be gaining weight, watch his diet, as this could affect his lifespan. Excess weight will put undue pressure on the heart, which can often be detected by a cough, but there can also be stress on other organs and limbs.

However, a cough need not necessarily be a heart problem: it could be worms. You should have maintained a regular worming routine throughout your dog's life, and an older dog should be

wormed annually. However, if your dog is old and in general ill-health, your vet will advise you whether or not worming would be wise.

Grooming sessions for the older Apso should be kept fairly short. 'Little and often' is the motto. Make certain your Apso is never allowed to get damp or cold, and, when he has been bathed, he should be kept in a pleasantly warm temperature for a good while afterwards.

Should your older Lhasa Apso's sight be failing, try not to move furniture or other household items any more than is necessary. If he knows where things are, even without seeing them properly, he will feel more confident, and accidents will be kept to a minimum.

A 'mishap' that can sometimes occur with an older dog is that he may be having increasing difficulty in controlling his water-works. There can be a whole variety of reasons for this and you should certainly consult your vet, especially if your dog has normally been clean in the house. If an old dog has an accident of this kind, do not scold him, for there is almost certainly a reason for this unintentional misdemeanour. Instead you should consider putting a thick wad of newspaper by the door, for he will probably be aware that he wants to go, but you may not be there to let him out, or he may simply not make it in time.

In general, I would recommend that a young puppy should not be introduced to the household while a dog is in the closing stages of his life, for the exuberant youngster may just be too much for him. But the older dog's personality will play a part in your decision, as will his ailments and your own domestic circumstances. What is certain is that if a younger dog comes to live with you all, the older animal must never have his nose pushed out and must be allowed plenty of time alone in which to relax and rest when needed. It goes without saying, that if you do decide to introduce another dog while your old dog is still alive, that you must take very special care that harmony reigns, for the old chap may decide to snap at the youngster if his antics get just too much.

LETTING GO

Sooner or later the inevitable time to part will come around. If you are lucky, your old dog will just pass away peacefully in his sleep, sparing you the pain and anguish of deciding whether or not the time has come to put him out of his suffering. But of all the dogs I have owned, I can count on one hand those who have died naturally this way. It is a mercy that vets are now able to prescribe some excellent pain-killing drugs, so that even if an ailment is serious and terminal, your dog can be kept free from pain.

Having a dog put to sleep

In time, you will be able to look back and remember all the happy times you spent with beloved Lhasa Apso. © Carol Ann Johnson

inevitably brings with it distress for the owner, but you must try not to show your dog how upset you are. There will be time for tears after he has gone. If possible, choose a vet with whom you are familiar, and whom your dog has come to know well; this will make that final visit easier for both of you. If your dog is in pain, he will probably associate the surgery with the place he goes to be relieved of his pain, and this is just how it will be. Alternatively, the vet will probably visit you at your home if you wish.

However difficult it may be, try to keep control of your emotions in front of your dog, and stay with him until he has been injected so that you can give him your reassurance as he goes finally to sleep. That sleep will usually come quickly and almost imperceptibly, so, after many years' faithful service, try not to

let him down at the last.

In most cases, you can leave final disposal of the body in the hands of your vet. The ashes will be returned to you and you may scatter them in your garden or keep them at home in a pretty urn or tidy box, as I do. Some pet crematoria offer the option of burying the ashes in their own grounds, with the erection of a plaque. Understandably there is a substantial cost for individual cremation, but for your peace of mind, I think it worthwhile.

On the unhappy subject of parting, you should also consider that your dog may outlive you, so it would be wise to make some provision for him in your will. Speak to your solicitor about how your dog can be included. This will give you peace of mind and you will know that you will have done your very best for your pet, right up to the last.

TRAINING AND SOCIALISATION

Chapter 6

When you decided to bring a Lhasa Apso into your life, you probably had dreams of how it was going to be: you envisaged living with a devoted companion that brought fun and happiness into your life, fitting in with everything you wanted to do. There is no doubt that you can achieve all this – and much more – with an Apso, but like anything that is worth having, you must be prepared to put in the work. A Lhasa Apso, regardless of whether he is a puppy or an adult, does not come ready trained, understanding exactly what you want and fitting perfectly into your lifestyle. An Apso has to learn his place in your family and he must discover what is acceptable behaviour.

We have a great starting point in that the breed has an outstanding temperament. The Lhasa Apso was bred first and foremost as a companion dog, and he wants nothing more than to be with people. He is also highly intelligent and very quick to learn. That means he will pick up bad habits as quickly as good habits, so you must obey the golden rule: start as you mean to go on.

THE FAMILY PACK

Dogs have been domesticated for some 14,000 years, but luckily for us, they have inherited and retained behaviour from their distant ancestor – the wolf. A Lhasa Apso may never have lived in the wild, but he is born with the survival skills and the mentality of a meat-eating predator who hunts in a pack. A wolf living in a pack owes its existence to mutual co-operation and an acceptance of a hierarchy, as this ensures both food and protection. A domesticated dog living in a family pack has exactly the same outlook. He wants food, companionship, and leadership – and it is your job to provide for these needs.

YOUR ROLE

Theories about dog behaviour and methods of training go in and out of fashion, but, in reality, nothing has changed from the day when wolves ventured in from the wild to join the family circle. The wolf (and equally the dog) accepts a subservient place in the family pack in return for food and protection. In a dog's eyes, you are his leader and he relies on you to make all the important decisions. This does not mean that you have to act like a dictator or a bully. You are accepted as a leader, without argument, as long as you have the right credentials.

The first part of the job is easy.

You are the provider and you are therefore respected because you supply food. In a Lhasa Apso's eyes, you must be the ultimate hunter, because a day never goes by when you cannot find food. The second part of the leader's job description is straightforward, but for some reason we find it hard to achieve. In order for a dog to accept his place in the family pack, he must respect his leader as the decision-maker. A low-ranking pack animal does not question authority; he is perfectly happy to see someone else shoulder the responsibility. Problems will only arise if you cut a poor figure as leader and the dog feels he should mount a challenge for the top-ranking role.

HOW TO BE A GOOD LEADER

There are a number of guidelines to follow to establish yourself in the role of leader in a way that your Lhasa Apso understands and respects. You may have chosen an Apso because he looks like a cuddly teddy bear – but do not be fooled! This is a dog with a strong, sometimes assertive, character, and he needs firm and consistent guidance. Remember, he is not a toy – he is a living, breathing animal with a mind of his own.

Have you got what it takes to be a firm, fair and consistent leader?
                                    © *Juliette Cunliffe*

When your puppy first arrives home, you may think you don't have to worry about training for a few months, but that would be a big mistake. The behaviour he learns as a puppy will continue throughout his adult life, which means that undesirable behaviour can be very difficult to rectify.

When your Lhasa Apso first arrives in his new home, follow these guidelines:

- **Keep it simple:** Decide on the rules you want your Apso to obey and always make it 100 per cent clear what is acceptable, and what is unacceptable, behaviour.

- **Be consistent:** If you are not consistent about enforcing rules, how can you expect your Apso to take you seriously? There is nothing worse than allowing your Lhasa Aso to jump on the sofa one moment and then scolding him the next time he does it because he is muddy. As far as the dog is concerned, he may as well try it on because he can't predict your reaction. Inconsistency leads to insecurity.

- **Get your timing right:** If you are rewarding your Lhasa Apso and equally if you are reprimanding him, you must respond within one to two seconds, otherwise the dog will not link his behaviour with your reaction (see page 91).

- **Read your dog's body language:** Find out how to read body language and facial expressions (see page 89) so that you understand your Apso's feelings and intentions.

- **Be aware of your own body language:** When you ask your Lhasa Apso to do something, do not bend over him and eyeball him. This could be seen as a direct challenge. Assert your authority by standing over him and keeping an upright posture. You can also help your dog to learn by using your body language to communicate with him. For example, if you want your dog to come to you, open your arms out and look inviting. If you want your dog to stay, use a hand signal (palm flat, facing the dog) so you are effectively 'blocking' his advance.

- **Tone of voice:** Dogs do not speak English; they learn by associating a word with the required action. However, they are very receptive to tone of voice, so you can use your voice to praise him or to correct undesirable behaviour. If you are pleased with your Lhasa Apso, praise him to the skies in a warm, happy voice. If you want to stop him raiding the bin, use a deep, stern voice when you say, "No".

- **Give one command only:** If you keep repeating a command, or keeping changing it, your Lhasa Apso will think you are babbling and will probably ignore you. If your Apso does not respond the first time you ask, make it simple by using a treat to lure him into position and then you

A dog will tune into body language more readily than into verbal communication.

can reward him for a correct response. The same applies to using your dog's name. Generally, we use a dog's name to get his attention. If you keep repeating the name, the likelihood is that your dog will 'tune out' because the use of his name has no special meaning.

- **Daily reminders:** A young, carefree Lhasa Apso is apt to forget his manners from time to time and an adolescent dog may attempt to challenge your authority (see page 102). Rather than coming down on your Lhasa Apso like a ton of

bricks when he does something wrong, try to prevent bad manners by daily reminders of good manners. For example:
  i. Do not let your dog barge ahead of you when you are going through a door.
  ii. Do not let him leap out of the car the moment you open the door (which could be potentially lethal, as well as being disrespectful).
  iii. Do not let him eat from your hand when you are at the table.
  iv. Do not let him 'win' a toy at the end of a play session and then make off with it. You 'own' his toys and you 'allow' him to play with them. Your Apso must learn to give up a toy when you ask.

UNDERSTANDING YOUR LHASA APSO

Body language is an important means of communication between dogs, which they use to make friends, to assert status and to avoid conflict. It is important to get on your dog's wavelength by understanding his body language and reading his facial expressions. This is not always easy with a long-coated breed that has a spectacular head fall, but most owners learn to read their own dogs, in a way that strangers might fail to do.

- A positive body posture and a

This Labrador puppy is slightly overwhelmed by the Apso greeting party – but it is clear that their intentions are non-threatening.

wagging tail indicate a happy, confident dog.

- A crouched body posture with ears back and tail down show that a dog is being submissive. A dog may do this when he is being told off or if a more assertive dog approaches him.
- A bold dog will stand as tall as he can, looking strong and alert. His ears will be forward and his tail will be held high.
- A playful dog will go down on his front legs while standing on his hind legs in a bow position. This friendly invitation says: "I'm no threat, let's play."
- A dominant, aggressive dog will meet other dogs with a hard stare. If he is challenged, he may bare his teeth and growl, and the corners of his mouth will be drawn forward. His ears will be forward and he will

appear tense in every muscle.
- A nervous dog will often show aggressive behaviour as a means of self-protection. If threatened, this dog will lower his head and flatten his ears. The corners of his mouth may be drawn back and he may bark or whine.

GIVING REWARDS

Why should your Lhasa Apso do as you ask? If you follow the guidelines given above, your Apso should respect your authority, but what about the time when he is playing with a new doggy friend or has found a really enticing scent? The answer is that you must always be the most interesting, the most attractive, and the most irresistible person in your Lhasa Apso's eyes. It would be nice to

think that you could achieve this by personality alone, but most of us need a little extra help. You need to find out what is the biggest reward for your dog. In most cases, a Lhasa Apso will be motivated to work for a food reward, although some can become obsessed with a particular toy. But whatever reward you use, make sure it is something that your dog really wants.

When you are teaching a dog a new exercise, you should reward your Lhasa Apso frequently. When he knows the exercise or command, reward him randomly so that he keeps on responding to you in a positive manner. If your dog does something extra special, like leaving his canine chum mid-play in the park, make sure he really knows how pleased you are by giving him a handful of treats or throwing his ball a few extra times. If he gets a bonanza reward, he is more likely to come back on future occasions because you have proved to be even more rewarding than his previous activity.

TOP TREATS

Some trainers grade treats depending on what they are asking the dog to do. A dog may get a low-grade treat, such as a piece of dry food, to reward good behaviour on a random basis, such as sitting when you open a door or allowing you to examine his teeth. But high-grade treats, which may be cooked liver, sausage or cheese, are reserved for training new exercises or for use in the park when you want a really good recall. Whatever type of treat you use, remember to subtract it from your Lhasa Apso's daily ration. Like all breeds, the Lhasa Apso will put on weight if he is fed too much or if he is given inappropriate food. Remember, fat dogs are lethargic, prone to health problems and will almost certainly have a shorter life expectancy, so reward your Apso, but always keep a check on his figure!

HOW DO DOGS LEARN?

It is not difficult to get inside your Lhasa Apso's head and understand how he learns, as it is not dissimilar to the way we learn. Dogs learn by conditioning: they find out that specific behaviours produce

To begin with, the dog must give his attention to the handler to earn a click.

specific consequences. This is known as operant conditioning or consequence learning. Consequences have to be immediate or clearly linked to the behaviour, as a dog sees the world in terms of action and result. Dogs will quickly learn if an action has a bad consequence or a good consequence.

Dogs also learn by association. This is known as classical conditioning or association

learning. It is the type of learning made famous by Pavlov's experiment with dogs. Pavlov presented dogs with food and measured their salivary response (how much they drooled). Then he rang a bell just before presenting the food. At first, the dogs did not salivate until the food was presented. But after a while they learnt that the sound of the bell meant that food was coming and so they salivated

THE CLICKER REVOLUTION

Karen Pryor pioneered the technique of clicker training when she was working with dolphins. It is very much a continuation of Pavlov's work and makes full use of association learning. Karen wanted to mark 'correct' behaviour at the precise moment it happened. She found it was impossible to toss a fish to a dolphin when it was in mid-air, when she wanted to reward it. Her aim was to establish a conditioned response so the dolphin knew that it had performed correctly and a reward would follow.

The solution was the clicker: a small matchbox-shaped training aid, with a metal tongue that makes a click when it is pressed. To begin with, the dolphin had to learn that a click meant that food was coming. The dolphin then learnt that it must 'earn' a click in order to get a reward. Clicker training has been used with many different animals, most particularly with dogs, and it has proved hugely successful. It is a great aid for pet owners and is also widely used by professional trainers who are training highly specialised skills.

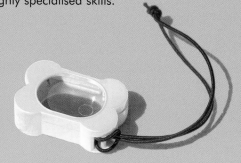

when they heard the bell. A dog needs to learn the association in order for it to have any meaning. For example, a dog that has never seen a lead before will be completely indifferent to it. A dog that has learnt that a lead means he is going for a walk will get excited the second he sees the lead; he has learnt to associate a lead with a walk.

BE POSITIVE
The most effective method of training dogs is to use their ability to learn by consequence and to teach that the behaviour you want produces a good consequence. For example, if you ask your Lhasa Apso to "Sit" and reward him with a treat, he will learn that it is worth his while to sit on command because it will lead to a reward. He is far more likely to repeat the behaviour and the behaviour will become stronger, because it results in a positive outcome. This method of training is known as positive reinforcement and it generally leads to a happy, co-operative dog that is willing to work and a handler who has fun training their dog.

The opposite approach is negative reinforcement. This is far less effective and often results in a poor relationship between dog and owner. In this method of training, you ask your Lhasa Apso to "Sit" and if he does not respond, you deliver a sharp yank on the training collar or push his rear to the ground. The dog learns that not responding to your command has a bad consequence and he may be less likely to ignore you in the future. However, it may well have a bad consequence for you, too. A dog that is treated in this way may associate harsh handling with the handler and become aggressive or fearful. Instead of establishing a pattern of willing co-operation, you are establishing a relationship built on coercion.

GETTING STARTED

As you train your Lhasa Apso you will develop your own techniques as you get to know what motivates him. You may decide to get involved with clicker training or you may prefer to go for a simple command-and-reward formula. It does not matter what form of training you use, as long as it is based on positive, reward-based methods.

There are a few important guidelines to bear in mind when you are training your Apso:

- Find a training area that is free from distractions, particularly when you are just starting out. A young dog is excitable and is easily distracted, so you need the training environment to be as neutral as possible.
- Keep training sessions short, especially with a young puppy that has a very short attention span.
- Do not train if you are in a bad mood or if you are on a tight schedule – the training session will be doomed to failure.
- If you are using a toy as a reward, make sure it is only available when you are training. In this way it has an added value for your Lhasa Apso.
- If you are using food treats, make sure they are bite-sized and easy to swallow; you don't want to hang about while your Apso chews on his treat.
- Do not attempt to train your Lhasa Apso after he has eaten, or soon after returning from exercise. He will either be too

It does not take him long to learn that a click means a reward will follow.

full up to care about food treats or too tired to concentrate.

- When you are training, move around your allocated area so that your dog does not think that an exercise can only be performed in one place.
- If your Lhasa Apso is finding an exercise difficult, try not to get frustrated. Go back a step and praise him for his effort. You will probably find he is more successful when you try again at the next training session.
- If a training session is not going well – either because you are in the wrong frame of mind or the dog is not focusing –

ask your Lhasa Apso to do something he finds easy (such as a trick he enjoys performing) and then you can reward him with a food treat or with a play with his favourite toy, ending the session on a happy, positive note.

- Do not train for too long. You need to end a training session on a high, with your Lhasa Apso wanting more, rather than making him sour by asking too much from him.

In the exercises that follow, clicker training is introduced and followed, but all the exercises will work without the use of a clicker.

INTRODUCING A CLICKER

This is dead easy, and the intelligent Lhasa Apso will learn about the clicker in record time! It can be combined with attention training, which is a very useful tool and can be used on many different occasions.

- Prepare some treats and go to an area that is free from distractions. Allow your Lhasa Apso to wander, and, when he stops to look at you, click and reward by throwing him a treat. This means he will not crowd you, but will go looking for the treat. Repeat a couple of times. If your Apso is very easily distracted, you may need to start this exercise with the dog on a lead.

- After a few clicks, your Lhasa Apso will understand that if he hears a click, he will get a treat. He must now learn that he must 'earn' a click. This time, when your Apso looks at you, wait a little longer before clicking and then reward him. If your Apso is on a lead but responding well, try him off the lead.

- When your Lhasa Apso is working for a click and giving you his attention, you can introduce a cue or command word, such as "Watch". Repeat a few times, using the cue. You now have a Lhasa Apso that understands the clicker and will give you his attention when you ask him to "Watch".

TRAINING EXERCISES

The Lhasa Apso is not a natural obedience dog in the sense that he will not respond like a Border Collie, for example, for the sheer love of working. However, training exercises mean more than getting your dog to perform specific tasks. You are interacting with him, enhancing and underlining your relationship with him so that he loves and respects you as his leader. You may not feel the need to work on all the following exercises, but training represents quality time with your Lhasa Apso, and this should never be under-estimated. In addition, the aim of every owner is to have a calm, well-behaved dog who will fit in with all family activities.

THE SIT

This is the easiest exercise to teach, so it is rewarding for both you and your Lhasa Apso.

- Choose a tasty treat and hold it just above your puppy's nose.

To begin with, lure your Apso into position. In time, he will respond to a verbal cue.

As he looks up at the treat, he will naturally go into the 'Sit'. As soon as he is in position, reward him.

- Repeat the exercise, and, when your pup understands what you want, introduce the "Sit" command.

- You can practise at mealtimes by holding out the bowl and waiting for your dog to sit. Most Lhasa Apsos learn this one very quickly!

THE DOWN

Work hard at this exercise because a reliable 'Down' is useful in many different situations, and an instant 'Down' can be a lifesaver.

- You can start with your dog in a 'Sit', or it is just as effective to teach it when the dog is standing. Hold a treat just below your puppy's nose and slowly lower it towards the ground. The treat acts as a lure and your puppy will follow it, first going down on his forequarters and then bringing his hindquarters down as he tries to get the treat.

- Make sure you close your fist around the treat and only reward your puppy with the treat when he is in the correct position. If your puppy is reluctant to go 'Down', you can apply gentle pressure on his shoulders to encourage him to go into the correct position.

- When your puppy is following the treat and going into position, introduce a verbal command.

This Apso has learnt to go into the Down position. He is waiting for a click, knowing a reward will follow.

- Build up this exercise over a period of time, each time waiting a little longer before giving the reward, so the puppy learns to stay in the 'Down' position.

THE RECALL

This is an important exercise if you are to give your Lhasa Apso the freedom he deserves. If your dog has a poor recall, you will be worried about letting him off lead for exercise – and this will have a detrimental effect on his lifestyle.

Hopefully, the breeder will have already started recall training by calling the puppies in from outside and rewarding them with some treats scattered on the floor.

But even if this has not been the case, you will find that a puppy arriving in his new home is highly responsive. His chief desire is to follow you and be with you. Capitalise on this from day one by getting your pup's attention and calling him to you in a bright, excited tone of voice.

- Practise in the garden. When your puppy is busy exploring, get his attention by calling his name. As he runs towards you, introduce the verbal command "Come". Make sure you sound happy and exciting, so your puppy wants to come to you. When he responds, give him lots of praise.

COMING WHEN CALLED

You can ask your Apso to "Sit" and "Wait".

The aim is to build up a really enthusiastic response to the Recall.

Give lots of encouragement as your Apso comes towards you.

- If your puppy is slow to respond, try running away a few paces, or jumping up and down. It doesn't matter how silly you look, the key issue is to get your puppy's attention and then make yourself irresistible!
- In a dog's mind, coming when called should be regarded as the best fun because he knows he is always going to be rewarded. Never make the mistake of telling your dog off, no matter how slow he is to respond, as you will undo all your previous hard work.
- When you call your Lhasa Apso to you, make sure he comes up close enough to be touched. He must understand that "Come" means that he should come right up to you, otherwise he will think that he can approach and then veer off when it suits him.
- When you are free running your dog, make sure you have his favourite toy or a pocket full of treats so you can reward him at intervals throughout the walk when you call him to you. Do not allow your dog to free run and only call him back at the end of the walk to clip on his lead. An intelligent Apso will soon realise that the recall means the end of his walk and then end of fun – so who can blame him for not wanting to come back?

TRAINING LINE
This is the equivalent of a very long lead, which you can buy at a pet store, or you can make your own with a length of rope. The training line is attached to your Lhasa Apso's collar and should be around 15 feet (4.5 metres) in length.

The purpose of the training line is to prevent your Lhasa Apso from disobeying you so that he never has the chance to get into bad habits. For example, when you call your Apso and he ignores you, you can immediately pick up the end of the training line and call him again. By picking up the line you will have attracted his attention and if you call him in an excited, happy

SECRET WEAPON

You can build up a strong recall by using another form of association learning. Buy a whistle and peep on it when you are giving your Lhasa Apso his food. You can choose the type of signal you want to give: two short peeps or one long whistle, for example. Within a matter of days, your dog will learn that the sound of the whistle means that food is coming.

Now transfer the lesson outside. Arm yourself with some tasty treats and the whistle. Allow your Lhasa Apso to run free in the garden, and, after a couple of minutes, use the whistle. The dog has already learnt to associate the whistle with food, so he will come towards you.

Immediately reward him with a treat and lots of praise. Repeat the lesson a few times in the garden, so you are confident that your dog is responding before trying it in the park. Make sure you always have some treats in your pocket when you go for a walk and your dog will quickly learn how rewarding it is to come to you.

voice, your Lhasa Apso will come to you. The moment he reaches you, give him a tasty treat so he is instantly rewarded for making the 'right' decision.

WALKING ON A LOOSE LEAD

This is a simple exercise, which baffles many dog owners. Although the Lhasa Apso is a small dog, he can be very bouncy and excitable, and he can quickly get into the habit of pulling on the lead or meandering from side to side as the whim takes him. In most cases, owners make the mistake of wanting to get on with the expedition rather that training the dog how to walk on a lead.

In this exercise, as with all lessons that you teach your Lhasa Apso, you must adopt a calm, determined, no-nonsense attitude so he knows that you mean business. However, do not become confrontational, as this will cut no ice with a Lhasa Apso. This is the type of dog that is happy to co-operate because he decides it is a good idea. He resents any degree of force or bullying and will simply dig his heels in and have nothing to do with you.

- In the early stages of lead training, allow your puppy to pick his route and follow him. He will get used to the feeling of being 'attached' to you and has no reason to put up any resistance.

- Next, find a toy or a tasty treat and show it to your puppy. Let him follow the treat/toy for a few paces and then reward him.

- Build up the amount of time your pup will walk with you, and, when he is walking nicely by your side, introduce the verbal command "Heel" or "Close". Give lots of praise when your pup is in the correct position.

- When your pup is walking alongside you, keep focusing his attention on you by using his name and then rewarding him when he looks at you. If it is going well, introduce some changes of direction.

- Do not attempt to take your

puppy out on the lead until you have mastered the basics at home. You need to be confident that your puppy accepts the lead and will focus his attention on you, when requested, before you face the challenge of a busy environment.

- If you are heading somewhere special, such as the park, your Lhasa Apso may try to pull or jump up because he is impatient to get there. If this happens, stop, call your dog to you and do not set off again until he is in the correct position. It may take time, but your Lhasa Apso will eventually realise that it is more productive to walk by your side, as this is the quickest way to get to the desired destination.

You want your Apso to walk on a loose lead, neither pulling ahead nor lagging behind.

STAYS

This may not be the most exciting exercise, but it is one of the most useful. There are many occasions when you want your Lhasa Apso to stay in position, even if it is only for a few seconds. The classic example is when you want your Lhasa Apso to stay in the back of the car until you have clipped on his lead. Some trainers use the verbal command "Stay" when the dog is to stay in position for an extended period of time and

"Wait" if the dog is to stay in position for a few seconds until you give the next command. Others trainers use a universal "Stay" to cover all situations. It all comes down to personal preference, and as long as you are consistent, your dog will understand the command he is given.

- Put your puppy in a 'Sit' or a 'Down' and use a hand signal (flat palm, facing the dog) to show he is to stay in position. Step a pace away from the dog. Wait a second, step back and reward him. If you have a lively pup, you may find it easier to train this exercise on the lead.

- Repeat the exercise, gradually increasing the distance you can leave your dog. When you return to your dog's side, praise him quietly and release him with a command, such as "OK".

- Remember to keep your body language very still when you are training this exercise, and avoid eye contact with your dog.

- You can also train this exercise at mealtimes, teaching your dog to "Wait" for a few seconds until you give him the go ahead to eat his food.

- Work on this exercise over a period of time and you will build up a really reliable 'Stay'.

SOCIALISATION

While your Lhasa Apso is mastering basic obedience exercises, there is other, equally important work to do with him. A Lhasa Apso is not only becoming a part of your home and family, he is becoming a member of the community. He needs to be able to live in the outside world, coping calmly with every new situation that comes his way. It is your job to introduce him to as many different experiences as possible and to encourage him to behave in an appropriate manner. The Lhasa Apso is a sound dog, but he is sometimes cautious. He needs time to assimilate new experiences so he can learn to take them in his stride.

In order to socialise your Lhasa Apso effectively, it is helpful to understand how his brain is developing and then you will get a perspective on how he sees the world.

CANINE SOCIALISATION
(Birth to 7 weeks)

This is the time when a dog learns how to be a dog. By interacting with his mother and his littermates, a young pup learns about leadership and submission. He learns to read body posture so that he understands the intentions of his mother and his siblings. A puppy that is taken away from his litter too early may always have behavioural problems with other dogs, either being fearful or aggressive.

SOCIALISATION PERIOD
(7 to 12 weeks)

This is the time to get cracking and introduce your Lhasa Apso puppy to as many different experiences as possible. This includes meeting different people, other dogs and animals, seeing new sights and hearing a range of sounds, from the vacuum cleaner to the roar of traffic.

Build up the Stay exercise in easy stages.

It may be that your Lhasa Apso has been reared in kennels. If this is the case, you must work even harder at this stage of his education. A puppy learns very quickly and what he learns will stay with him for the rest of his life. This is the best time for a puppy to move to a new home, as he is adaptable and ready to form deep bonds.

FEAR-IMPRINT PERIOD
(8 to 11 weeks)

This occurs during the socialisation period and it can be the cause of problems if it is not handled carefully. If a pup is exposed to a frightening or painful experience, it will lead to lasting impressions. Obviously,

you will attempt to avoid frightening situations, such as your pup being bullied by a mean-spirited older dog, or a firework going off, but you cannot always protect your puppy from the unexpected. If your pup has a nasty experience, the best plan is to make light of it and distract him by offering him a treat or a game. The pup will take the lead from you and will be reassured that there is nothing to worry about. If you mollycoddle him and sympathise with him, he is far more likely to retain the memory of his fear.

SENIORITY PERIOD
(12 to 16 weeks)

During this period, your Lhasa Apso puppy starts to cut the apron strings and becomes more independent. He will test out his status to find out who is the pack leader: him or you. Bad habits, such as play biting, which may have been seen as endearing a few weeks earlier, should be firmly discouraged. Remember to use positive, reward-based training, but make sure your puppy knows that you are the leader and must be respected.

During the fear imprint period, a puppy may retain the memory of a bad experience if it is not handled correctly.

SECOND FEAR-IMPRINT PERIOD (6 to 14 months)

This period is not as critical as the first fear-imprint period, but it should still be handled carefully. During this time your Lhasa Apso may appear apprehensive, or he may show fear of something familiar. You may feel as if you have taken a backwards step, but if you adopt a calm, positive manner, your Apso will see that there is nothing to be frightened of. Do not make your dog confront the thing that frightens him. Simply distract his attention, and give him something else to think about, such as obeying a simple command, such as "Sit" or "Down". This will give you the opportunity to praise and reward your dog and will help to boost his confidence.

YOUNG ADULTHOOD AND MATURITY (1 to 4 years)

The timing of this phase depends on the size of the dog: the bigger the dog, the later it is. This period coincides with a dog's increased size and strength, mental as well as physical. Some dogs, particularly those with a dominant nature, will test your leadership again and may become aggressive towards other dogs. Firmness and continued training are essential at this time, so that your Lhasa Apso accepts his status in the family pack.

IDEAS FOR SOCIALISATION

When you are socialising your Lhasa Apso, you want him to experience as many different situations as possible. However, do not be in too much of a hurry to swamp your puppy with challenging environments until he has built up his confidence. It is a good idea to train your Apso puppy just to sit quietly and listen to the traffic sounds around him. When you feel he is sufficiently confident, you could take him along to places where dogs are welcome such as an outdoor market or garden centre, where he will encounter a range of different sights and sounds. Busy high streets can come later when you are fully confident that your puppy will not back away from things like pushchairs and prying children's fingers. It's a big, wide world out there, so allow your puppy plenty of time to adjust.

If you are taking on a rescued dog and have little knowledge of his background, it is important to work through a programme of socialisation. A young puppy soaks up new experiences like a sponge, but an older dog can still learn. If a rescued dog shows fear or apprehension, treat him in exactly the same way as you would treat a youngster who is going through the second fear-imprint period.

As your puppy is growing up, or as your adult dog settles into his new home, try out the following ideas for socialisation:

- Accustom your puppy to household noises, such as the vacuum cleaner, the television and the washing machine.
- Ask visitors to come to the door, wearing different types of clothing – for example, wearing a hat, a long raincoat, or carrying a stick or an umbrella.
- If you do not have children at home, make sure your Lhasa Apso has a chance to meet and play with them. Go to a local park and watch children in the play area. You will not be able to take your Lhasa Apso inside the play area, but he will see children playing and will get used to their shouts of excitement.
- Attend puppy classes. These are designed for puppies between the ages of 12 to 20 weeks and give puppies a chance to play and interact together in a controlled, supervised environment. Your vet will have details of a local class.
- Take a walk around some quiet streets, such as a residential area, so your Lhasa Apso can get used to the sound of traffic. As he becomes more confident, progress to busier areas. Remember: your lead is like a live wire, and your feelings will travel directly to

A young puppy will soak up new experiences like a sponge.

your Lhasa Apso. Assume a calm, confident manner and your puppy will take the lead from you and have no reason to be fearful.

- Go to a railway station. You don't have to get on a train if you don't need to, but your Lhasa Apso will have the chance to experience trains, people wheeling luggage, loudspeaker announcements and going up and down stairs and over railway bridges.
- If you live in the town, plan a trip to the country. You can

enjoy a day out and provide an opportunity for your Lhasa Apso to see livestock, such as sheep, cattle and horses.

- One of the best places for socialising a dog is at a country fair. There will be crowds of people, livestock in pens, tractors, bouncy castles, fairground rides and food stalls.
- When your dog is over 20 weeks of age, locate a training class for adult dogs. You may find that your local training class has both puppy and adult classes.

The adolescent Lhasa Apso may temporarily 'forget' all the lessons you have taught him.

THE ADOLESCENT LHASA APSO

It happens to every dog – and every owner. One minute you have an obedient, well-behaved youngster and the next you have an adolescent who appears to have forgotten everything he ever learnt.

The Lhasa Apso is a long-lived breed, and it takes time for them to reach full maturity. A male will still be as playful as a puppy at two years of age, not maturing until he is three years old. Most Lhasa Apso owners would agree that a male is not 'grown up' until he is four year old.

As with most breeds, the female

Lhasa Apso matures more quickly than the male. A bitch will have her first season between six months and 12 months of age. If she is bred from (and if she is living with others dogs), it is very noticeable that a bitch will move up the pecking order after she has had a litter.

An adolescent Lhasa Apso, whether male or female, will try to test boundaries. This is an intelligent dog who knows how to get his own way, so you must be on hand to lay down firm guidelines. It is all too easy to allow a dog to step out of line because his behaviour is funny or cute, or because it does not seem

to matter. However, your Lhasa Apso will be quick to take advantage of your 'lenience', and his behaviour may become unacceptable.

This can be a trying time, but it is important to retain a sense of perspective. Look at the situations from the dog's viewpoint and respond to uncharacteristic behaviour with firmness and consistency. Just like a teenager, an adolescent Lhasa Apso feels the need to challenge the status quo. But if you show that you are a firm and consistent leader (see page 87) and are quick to reward good behaviour, your Lhasa Apso will be happy to accept you as his protector and provider.

WHEN THINGS GO WRONG

Positive, reward-based training has proved to be the most effective method of teaching dogs, but what happens when your Lhasa Apso does something wrong and you need to show him that his behaviour is unacceptable? The old-fashioned school of dog training used to rely on the powers of punishment and negative reinforcement. A dog who raided the bin, for example, was smacked. Now we have learnt that it is not only unpleasant and cruel to hit a dog, it is also ineffective. If you hit a dog for stealing, he is more than likely to see *you* as the bad consequence of stealing, so he may raid the bin again, but probably not when you are around. If he raided the bin some time before you discovered

TRAINING CLUBS

There are lots of training clubs to choose from. Your vet will probably have details of clubs in your area, or you can ask friends who have dogs if they attend a club. Alternatively, use the internet to find out more information. But how do you know if the club is any good?

Before you take your dog, ask if you can go to a class as an observer and find out the following:

- What experience does the instructor(s) have?
- Do they have experience with Lhasa Apsos?
- Is the class well organised and are the dogs reasonably quiet? (A noisy class indicates an unruly atmosphere, which will not be conducive to learning.)
- Are there are a number of classes to suit dogs of different ages and abilities?
- Are positive, reward-based training methods used?
- Does the club train for the Good Citizen Scheme (see page 109)?

If you are not happy with the training club, find another one. An inexperienced instructor who cannot handle a number of dogs in a confined environment can do more harm than good.

it, he will be even more confused by your punishment, as he will not relate your response to his 'crime'.

A more commonplace example is when a dog fails to respond to a recall in the park. When the dog eventually comes back, the owner puts the dog on the lead and goes straight home to punish the dog for his poor response. Unfortunately, the dog will have a different interpretation. He does not think: "I won't ignore a recall command because the bad consequence is the end of my play in the park." He thinks: "Coming to my owner resulted in the end of playtime – therefore coming to my owner has a bad consequence, so I won't do that again."

There are a number of strategies to tackle undesirable behaviour –

and they have nothing to do with harsh handling.

Ignoring bad behaviour
The Lhasa Apso is an independent-minded dog and undesirable behaviour in a youngster is often the result of an owner failing to give sufficient guidance. For example, a young Lhasa Apso that barks when you are preparing his food is showing his impatience and is attempting to train you, rather than the other way round. He believes he can change a situation simply by making a noise – and even if he does not get his food any quicker, he is enjoying the attention he is getting when you shout at him to tell him to be quiet. He is still getting attention, so why inhibit his behaviour?

In this situation, the best and most effective response is to ignore your Lhasa Apso. Suspend food preparations and get on with another task, such as washing up. Do not go near the food or the food bowl again until your Lhasa Apso is calm and quiet. Repeat this on every occasion when your Apso barks and he will soon learn that barking is non-productive. He is not rewarded with your attention – or with getting food. It will not take long for him to realise that being quiet is the most effective strategy. In this scenario, you have not only taught your Lhasa Apso to be quiet when you are preparing his food, you have also earned his respect because you have taken control of the situation.

Stopping bad behaviour

There are occasions when you want to call an instant halt to whatever it is your Lhasa Apso is doing. He may have just jumped on the sofa, or you may have caught him red-handed in the rubbish bin. He has already committed the 'crime', so your aim is to stop him and to redirect his attention. You can do this by using a deep, firm tone of voice to say, "No", which will startle him, and then call him to you in a bright, happy voice. If necessary, you can attract him with a toy or a treat. The moment your Lhasa Apso stops the undesirable behaviour and comes towards you, you can reward his good behaviour. You can back this up by running through a couple of simple exercises, such as a 'Sit' or a 'Down', and rewarding with treats. In this way, your Lhasa Apso focuses his attention on you and sees you as the greatest source of reward and pleasure.

In a more extreme situation, when you want to interrupt undesirable behaviour and you know that a simple "No" will not do the trick, you can try something a little more dramatic. If you get a can and fill it with pebbles, it will make a really loud noise when you shake it or throw it. The same effect can be achieved with purpose-made training discs. The dog will be startled and stop what he is doing. Even better, the dog will

If your Apso breaks the rules, do not become confrontational. Call him to you, and ask him to do a simple exercise, such as asking for a "Sit" so you can reward his 'good' behaviour.

not associate the unpleasant noise with you. This gives you the perfect opportunity to be the nice guy, calling the dog to you and giving him lots of praise.

PROBLEM BEHAVIOUR

If you have trained your Lhasa Apso from puppyhood, survived his adolescence and established yourself as a fair and consistent leader, you will end up with a brilliant companion dog. The Lhasa Apso is a well-balanced, adaptable dog, who rarely has hang-ups if he has been correctly reared and socialised. Most Lhasa Apsos are affectionate and fun-loving, and thrive on spending time with their owners.

The most common cause of problem behaviour among Lhasa Apsos is more to do with over-indulgent owners. The owner who sees his dog as a child substitute will end up with a spoilt dog who demands attention and sees no point in co-operating. This dog is not happy because he has got his own way; he often has a troubled life, as he has been forced to take on the role as decision-maker.

Fortunately, behavioural problems are rare, but it may be that you may have taken on older Apso that has established problems. If you are worried about your Lhasa Apso and feel out of your depth, do not delay in seeking professional help. This is readily available, usually through a referral from your vet, or you can find out additional information on the internet (see Appendices for web addresses). An animal behaviourist will have experience in tackling problem behaviour and will be able to help both you and your dog.

RESENTMENT OVER HANDLING/GROOMING

The Lhasa Apso is a long-coated, high-maintenance breed that requires a lot of hands-on attention throughout his life. He needs bathing, daily grooming, and dental care is a must. A well-raised Lhasa Apso, who has been used to grooming and handling from an early age, will accept this without resentment. In fact, most Apsos positively enjoy grooming sessions, seeing them as a time when they spend time with their owners.

However, a Lhasa Apso who has not been well handled may resent the constant attention that he needs. This may be because an owner has not spent enough time working with the dog and getting him used to grooming and health care procedures gradually, so that he does not become stressed. Or it may be that a dog has had a bad experience – the coat may have become matted, and grooming was therefore uncomfortable – so the dog is now concerned that he may suffer pain when he is put on the grooming table.

The most obvious strategy is to prevent this situation occurring in the following ways:

- Start handling as soon as your puppy arrives home, and reward him when he co-operates.
- If he struggles, hold him gently, talking to him calmly to reassure him. In a few moments, he will see that struggling does not work, and he will learn to relax.
- Keep grooming sessions short and positive so that they are a pleasurable experience for both of you.

If your Lhasa Apso has got into bad habits and resents being groomed, you will have to start from scratch:
- Spend time stroking and gently

If your Apso has experienced pain or discomfort when being brushed or combed, he may start to dread grooming sessions

massaging your dog so that he likes the feel of your hands and learns to relax.
- Start using the brush and try a few strokes, rewarding with a tasty treat when he co-operates. At this stage, you are not trying to 'groom' your dog, you are simply teaching him that grooming does not hurt, and he is rewarded when he sits still and accepts the procedure. Keep the first few sessions very short so he does not become worried or restless.
- Build up the amount of time your dog spends on the grooming table. It may help if you have a pot of treats within his eyesight so he can 'see' the reward and understand that he must co-operate with you to

earn it. If you have a helper, perhaps they could distract the dog and get his attention while you groom the coat.

Getting your Lhasa Apso to accept a full grooming session will take time and patience, but, remember, this is an intelligent dog who is quick to evaluate a situation. Once he understands that grooming is not painful or uncomfortable, he will start to relax – and working for rewards will encourage him to accept all procedure.

RESOURCE GUARDING
If you have trained and socialised your Lhasa Apso correctly, he will know his place in the family pack and will have no desire to

challenge your authority. If you have taken on a rescued dog who has not been trained and socialised, or if you have let your adolescent Lhasa Apso become over-assertive, you may find you have problems with a dog who is constantly pushing the boundaries. This may be expressed in different types of behaviour, which include the following:

- Showing lack of respect for your personal space. For example, your dog will barge through doors ahead of you or jump up at you.
- Ignoring basic obedience commands.
- Showing no respect to younger members of the family, pushing amongst them and completely ignoring them.
- Aggression towards people or other dogs (see page 108).

However, the most common behaviour displayed by a Lhasa Apso who has ideas above his station is resource guarding. This may take a number of different forms:

- Getting up on to the sofa or your favourite armchair and growling when you tell him to get back on the floor.
- Becoming possessive over a toy,

An Apso may become obsessed by a toy and resent giving it up.

or guarding his food bowl by growling when you get too close.
- Growling when anyone approaches his bed or when anyone gets too close to where he is lying.

In each of these scenarios, the Lhasa Apso has something he values and he aims to keep it. He does not have sufficient respect for you, his human leader, to give up what he wants and he is 'warning' you to keep away.

If you see signs of your Lhasa Apso behaving in his way, you must work at lowering his status so that he realises that you are the leader and he must accept your authority. Although you

need to be firm, you also need to use positive training methods so that your Lhasa Apso is rewarded for the behaviour you want. In this way, his 'correct' behaviour will be strengthened and repeated.

Do not become confrontational. As discussed previously, the Lhasa Apso will start playing 'mind games' with you and will become more difficult to handle. Keep it simple and keep it positive so that your Lhasa Apso 'decides' your way is the best way.

There are a number of steps you can take to lower your Lhasa Apso's status. They include:

- Go back to basics and hold daily training sessions. Make sure you have some really tasty treats. Run through all the training exercises you have taught your Lhasa Apso. Remember, boredom is often the key to undesirable behaviour. By giving your Apso things to do, you are providing mental stimulation and you have the opportunity to make a big fuss of him and reward him when he does well. This will help to reinforce the message that you are the leader and that it is rewarding to do as you ask.

- Teach your Lhasa Apso something new; this can be as simple as learning a trick, such as shaking paws. Having something new to think about will mentally stimulate your Apso and he will benefit from interacting with you.

- Be 100 per cent consistent with all house rules – your Lhasa Apso must never sit on the sofa and you must *never* allow him to jump up at you.

- If your Lhasa Apso is becoming possessive over a particular toy, the best strategy is to remove it from the equation. In fact, it may be a good idea to remove all toys, otherwise your Apso may simply find a new 'favourite' to guard. Toys should be reserved strictly for training sessions and play sessions when you are interacting with your Lhasa Apso. In this way you control his behaviour with toys, and you decide when he is allowed access to them. Your Lhasa Apso will have increased respect for you because you 'own' his toys, and he will put a high value on the times he is allowed to play with his toys when you are supervising him. He has fun playing and interacting with you, but the game is over – and the toy is given up – when you say so.

- If your Lhasa Apso has been guarding his food bowl, put the bowl down empty and drop in a little food at a time. Periodically stop dropping in the food and tell your Lhasa Apso to "Sit" and "Wait". Give

You need to teach your dog that you "own' his toys, and he must give them up on request.

it a few seconds and then reward him by dropping in more food. This shows your Lhasa Apso that you are the provider of the food and he can only eat when you allow him to.

- Make sure the family eats before you feed your Lhasa Apso Some trainers advocate eating in front of the dog (maybe just a few bites from a biscuit) before starting a training session, so the dog appreciates your elevated status.

- Do not let your Lhasa Apso barge through doors ahead of you or leap from the back of the car before you release him. You may need to put your dog

on the lead and teach him to "Wait" at doorways and then reward him for letting you go through first.

It will not take long for the clever Lhasa Apso to work out that co-operation means lots of rewards and increased time interacting with his family. If, however, you feel you are not making progress, do not delay in seeking professional help.

SEPARATION ANXIETY
A Lhasa Apso should be brought up to accept short periods of separation from his owner so that he does not become anxious. A new puppy should be left for short periods on his own, ideally

in a crate where he cannot get up to any mischief. It is a good idea to leave him with a boredom-busting toy so he will be happily occupied in your absence. When you return, do not rush to the crate and make a huge fuss. Wait a few minutes, and then calmly go to the crate and release your dog, telling him how good he has been. If this scenario is repeated a number of times, your Lhasa Apso will soon learn that being left on his own is no big deal.

Problems with separation anxiety are most likely to arise if you take on a rescued dog who has major insecurities. You may also find that your Lhasa Apso hates being left if you have failed to accustom him to short periods of isolation when he was growing up. Separation anxiety is expressed in a number of ways and all are equally distressing for both dog and owner. An anxious dog who is left alone may bark and whine continuously, urinate and defecate, and may be extremely destructive.

There are a number of steps you can take when attempting to solve this problem.

- Put up a baby-gate between adjoining rooms and leave your dog in one room while you are in the other room. Your dog will be able to see you and hear you, but he is learning to cope without being right next

If a Lhasa Apso is not used to spending periods on his own, he may become anxious.
© *Juliette Cunliffe*

to you. Build up the amount of time you can leave your dog in easy stages.
- Buy some boredom-busting toys and fill them with some tasty treats. Whenever you leave your dog, give him a food-filled toy so that he is busy while you are away.
- If you have not used a crate before, it is not too late to start. Make sure the crate is cosy and train your Lhasa Apso to get used to going in his crate while you are in the same room. Gradually build up the amount of time he spends in the crate and then start leaving the room for short periods. When you return, do not make a fuss of your dog. Leave him for five or ten minutes before releasing him, so that he gets

used to your comings and goings.
- Pretend to go out, putting on your coat and jangling keys, but do not leave the house. An anxious dog often becomes hyped up by the ritual of leaving and this will help to desensitize him.
- When you go out, leave a radio or a TV on. Some dogs are comforted by hearing voices and background noise when they are left alone.
- Try to make your absences as short as possible when you are first training your dog to accept being on his own. When you return, do not fuss your dog, rushing to his crate to release him. Leave him for a few minutes and when you go to him, remain calm and relaxed so that he does not become hyped up with a huge greeting.

If you take these steps, your dog should become less anxious, and, over a period of time, you should be able to solve the problem.

AGGRESSION
Aggression is a complex issue, as there are different causes and the behaviour may be triggered by numerous factors. It may be directed towards people, but far more commonly it is directed towards other dogs. Aggression in dogs may be the result of:
- Dominance (see page 104).
- Defensive behaviour: This may be induced by fear, pain or punishment.
- Territory: A dog may become

aggressive if strange dogs or people enter his territory (which is generally seen as the house and garden).

- Intra-sexual issues: This is aggression between sexes – male-to-male or female-to-female.
- Parental instinct: A mother dog may become aggressive if she is protecting her puppies.

The Lhasa Apso should not have a hint of aggression in his make-up, so if you see any signs of antagonism towards other dogs – or worse still, towards people – you know there must be an underlying cause. The first step is to get you Lhasa Apso checked by a vet to eliminate any physical causes for his behaviour

If dominance is the underlying cause, you can try the measures outlined above. Equally, if your dog has been poorly socialised, you can try to make up for lost time and work with other dogs of sound temperament in controlled situations. But if you are concerned about your dog's behaviour, you would be well advised to call in professional help. If the aggression is directed towards people, you should seek immediate advice. This behaviour can escalate very quickly and could lead to disastrous consequences.

NEW CHALLENGES
If you enjoy training your Lhasa

If you and your Apso are enjoying training, why not have a go at one of the dog sports on offer?

Apso, you may want to try one of the many dog sports that are now on offer. In the UK, there is a tendency to think that some breeds cannot compete in the canine disciplines because they do not have a suitable temperament for training. While it is true that some breeds, such as the Border Collie and the German Shepherd Dog, are naturals, there is no reason why you should not have a go – you may even surprise yourself! The most important point to remember is that all training must be positive, and you should only continue if your Lhasa Apso is enjoying what he is doing.

GOOD CITIZEN SCHEME
This is a scheme run by the Kennel Club in the UK and the

American Kennel Club in the USA. The schemes promote responsible ownership and help you to train a well-behaved dog who will fit in with the community. The schemes are excellent for all pet owners, and the Lhasa Apso should have no problems tackling the various exercises. The KC and the AKC schemes vary in format. In the UK there are three levels: bronze, silver and gold, with each test becoming progressively more demanding. In the AKC scheme there is a single test.

Some of the exercises include:

- Walking on a loose lead among people and other dogs.
- Recall amid distractions.
- A controlled greeting where dogs stay under control while their owners meet.
- The dog allows all-over grooming and handling by his owner, and also accepts being handled by the examiner.
- Stays, with the owner in sight and then out of sight.
- Food manners, allowing the owner to eat without begging and taking a treat on command.
- Sendaway – sending the dog to his bed.

The tests are designed to show the control you have over your dog and his ability to respond correctly and remain calm in all situations. The Good Citizen Scheme is taught at most training

Showing is highly competitive at the top level.

- **Recall:** This may be when the handler is stationary or on the move.
- **Retrieve:** This may be a dumbbell or any article chosen by the judge.
- **Sendaway:** The dog is sent to a designated spot and must go into an instant 'Down' until he is recalled by the handler.
- **Stays:** The dog must stay in the 'Sit' and in the 'Down' for a set amount of time. In advanced classes, the handler is out of sight.
- **Scent:** The dog must retrieve a single cloth from a pre-arranged pattern of cloths that has his owner's scent, or, in advanced classes, the judge's scent. There may also be decoy cloths.
- **Distance control.** The dog must execute a series of moves ('Sit', 'Stand', 'Down') without moving from his position and with the handler at a distance.

clubs. For more information, log on to the Kennel Club or AKC website (see Appendices).

SHOWING

The Lhasa Apso is a highly glamorous breed, and nothing looks better than seeing an Apso in full coat, showing to perfection. However, the show world is highly competitive, and it takes a lot of dedication to reach the top.

You will need to spend long hours learning how to present your Lhasa Apso for the show ring, and you will also need to teach him how to behave in the ring. Many training clubs hold ringcraft classes, which are run by experienced showgoers. At these classes, you will learn how to handle your dog in the ring and you will also find out about rules,

procedures and show ring etiquette.

The best plan is to start off at some small, informal shows where you can practise and learn the tricks of the trade before graduating to bigger shows.

COMPETITIVE OBEDIENCE

The Lhasa Apso is not known for competing in obedience, but if you are interested in the discipline, and do not get too obsessed about trying for clockwork precision, you may enjoy teaching the exercises that are required.

They include the following:

- **Heelwork:** Dog and handler must complete a set pattern on and off the lead, which includes left turns, right turns, about turns and changes of pace.

Even though competitive obedience requires accuracy, make sure you make it fun for your Lhasa Apso, with lots of praise and rewards so that you motivate him to do his best. Many training clubs run advanced classes for those who want to compete in obedience, or you can hire the services of a professional trainer for one-on-one sessions.

AGILITY

This fun sport has grown enormously in popularity over the past few years. All types of dog can compete, ranging from pedigree to non-pedigree, and the classes are divided into small, medium and large, depending on the dog's size. If you fancy having a go, make sure you have good control over your Lhasa Apso and keep him slim. Agility is a very physical sport, which demands fitness from both dog and handler.

In agility competitions, each dog must complete a set course over a series of obstacles, which include:

- Jumps (upright hurdles and long jump, varying in height – small, medium and large, depending on the size of the dog)
- Weaves
- A-frame
- Dog walk
- Seesaw
- Tunnels (collapsible and rigid)
- Tyre

Dogs may compete in Jumping classes, with jumps, tunnels and weaves, or in Agility classes, which have the full set of equipment. Faults are awarded for poles down on the jumps, missed contact points on the A-frame, dog walk and seesaw, and refusals. If a dog takes the wrong course, he is eliminated. The winner is the dog that completes

Even if you do not want to compete, your Lhasa Apso will enjoy learning some tricks that he can show off when visitors come round.

the course in the fastest time with no faults. As you progress up the levels, courses become progressively harder with more twists, turns and changes of direction.

If you want to get involved in Agility, you will need to find a club that specialises in the sport (see Appendices). You will not be allowed to start training until your Lhasa is 12 months old and you cannot compete until he is 18 months old. This rule is for the protection of the dog, who may suffer injury if he puts strain on bones and joints while he is still growing.

DANCING WITH DOGS

This sport is relatively new, but it is becoming increasingly popular. It is very entertaining to watch, but it is certainly not as simple as it looks. To perform a choreographed routine to music with your Lhasa Apso demands a huge amount of training.

Dancing with dogs is divided into two categories: heelwork to music and canine freestyle. In heelwork to music, the dog must work closely with his handler and show a variety of close 'heelwork' positions. In canine freestyle, the routine can be more flamboyant, with the dog working at a distance from the handler and performing spectacular tricks. Routines are judged on style and presentation, content and accuracy.

SUMMING UP

The Lhasa Apso is a breed apart – he is has so much to offer. He is glamorous, intelligent, alert and watchful. He is a loyal and loving – and so full of fun that he is a constant source of entertainment. Make sure you keep your half of the bargain: spend time socialising and training your Lhasa Apso so that you can be proud to take him anywhere, and he will always be a credit to you.

© Carol Ann Johnson

THE PERFECT LHASA APSO

Chapter 7

The Perfect Lhasa Apso is a bold statement – in fact, very bold – for, in truth, there is no perfect dog in any breed. Nonetheless, perfection is what all good breeders strive for, and to do this they aim to breed puppies that will grow into adults that adhere as closely as possible to the Kennel Club Breed Standard.

WHAT IS A BREED STANDARD?

A Breed Standard is effectively a picture of a breed, painted in words. But, of course, every individual will interpret a picture

HEALTH AND FITNESS FOR PURPOSE

In January 2009 the English Kennel Club revised its Breed Standards and introduced the following clause, which is worthy of note:

"A Breed Standard is the guideline which describes the ideal characteristics, temperament and appearance of a breed and ensures that the breed is fit for function. Absolute soundness is essential. Breeders and judges should at all times be careful to avoid obvious conditions or exaggerations which would be detrimental in any way to the health, welfare or soundness of this breed. From time to time certain conditions or exaggerations may be considered to have the potential to affect dogs in some breeds adversely, and judges and breeders are requested to refer to the Kennel Club website for details of any such current issues. If a feature or quality is desirable, it should only be present in the right measure."

slightly differently, and so it is with people's perception of dogs and the way in which a Standard is interpreted. If we all saw Lhasa Apsos in the very same light, the same dog would always be the top winner at shows, and this is certainly not the case.

Different breeders and judges lay more emphasis on certain traits that they consider the most important, but basically we are all aiming to breed and, hopefully, to judge dogs that most closely meet the Standard as set down by the Kennel Club. Breeding with the Breed Standard closely in our mind's eye means that we are aiming to breed a Lhasa Apso as opposed to any other breed of dog, for each breed's Standard is different.

Breed Standards vary slightly from country to country.

Essentially all the Breed Standards are roughly the same, but there are slight differences such as the wording regarding size, which differs in the USA, and the word 'chary', which was altered to 'aloof' in the UK over 20 years ago. Another important difference between the three Standards is that in the US the bite may still be level, whereas this no longer applies to the English and FCI Standards. The Standards are also laid out in slightly different ways, with different sub-headings, added to which the English Kennel Club's adaptation of the Standard to tie in with its recent policy of 'Fitness For Purpose' has brought about other changes, which can be noted as you compare each section of the Standard as applicable to each country below.

ANALYSIS AND INTERPRETATION

UK
GENERAL APPEARANCE
Well balanced, sturdy, heavily coated, without excess.

CHARACTERISTICS
Gay and assertive.

TEMPERAMENT
Alert, steady but somewhat aloof with strangers.

USA
CHARACTER
Gay and assertive, but chary of strangers.

FCI
CHARACTERISTICS
The Apso should give the appearance of a well-balanced, solid dog. Gay and assertive, but chary of strangers. Free and jaunty in movement.

Under 'General Appearance', a picture is conjured up of a dog that is neither extreme nor exaggerated, and yet does not have the delicate bone of some of the Toy breeds. Lhasa Apsos are in the Utility Group in Britain, Non-Sporting in the USA, but do fall into the Toy Group in just a few countries. This is a heavily coated breed, something that will be discussed in more depth later on.

From 'Characteristics' and 'Temperament' we learn a lot about the Lhasa Apso in just a few short words. "Gay" indicates cheerful, happy and full of fun,

The Lhasa Apso is a well balanced solid dog, which sets it aside from the more delicate Toy breeds.   © *Carol Ann Johnson*

whilst "assertive" tells us that the Lhasa Apso has strength of character; indeed, he is usually capable of showing other dogs exactly who is boss! By being "alert" the breed is quick to see and to act on what he has seen; he is watchful and always ready to deal with anything that indicates danger.

Although steady, he is also aloof with strangers, so although his temperament is well controlled, he can be rather 'stand-offish' with those he does not know. A Lhasa Apso should not bound up to people he doesn't know, smothering them with affection, but on the other hand he should not be aggressive toward them. A friendly character can certainly be an added bonus in the show ring, but it is not really what this breed is all about.

It is worth mentioning again that in the UK Standard, the word "aloof" replaced the word "chary" in the mid-1980s, the worry being that in a dog now destined for the show ring, this side of his character should not be allowed to become overly cautious.

The heavy head furnishings are a feature of the breed.
© *Carol Ann Johnson*

UK

HEAD AND SKULL

Head furnishings with fall over eyes, but not affecting the dog's ability to see, good whiskers and beard. Skull moderately narrow, falling away behind eyes, not quite flat, but not domed or apple headed. Straight foreface with medium stop. Nose black. Muzzle about 4 cms (1.5 ins), but not square; length from tip of nose roughly one-third total length from nose to back of skull.

EYES

Dark. Medium size, frontally placed, oval, neither large nor full, nor small and sunk. No white showing at base or top.

EARS

Pendant, heavily feathered.

MOUTH

Upper incisors close just inside lower i.e. reverse scissor bite. Incisors in a broad and as straight a line as possible. Full dentition desirable.

USA

HEAD

Heavy head furnishings with good fall over eyes, good whiskers and beard; skull narrow, falling away behind the eyes in a marked degree, not quite flat, but not domed or apple-shaped; straight foreface of fair length. Nose black, the length from tip of nose to eye to be roughly about one-third of the total length from nose to back of skull.

EYES

Dark brown, neither very large and full, nor very small and sunk.

The Lhasa Apso has extremely long eyelashes which stop hair going into the eyes.

The eyes are medium-sized and frontally placed.
© Carol Ann Johnson

EARS
Pendant, heavily feathered.

MOUTH AND MUZZLE
The preferred bite is either level or slightly undershot. Muzzle of medium length; a square muzzle is objectionable.

FCI
HEAD AND SKULL
Heavy head furnishings with good fall over the eyes, good whiskers and beard.
Skull moderately narrow, falling away behind the eyes in a marked degree; not quite flat, but not domed or apple shaped.
Straight foreface, with medium stop. Nose black. Muzzle about 1.5 inches long, but not square; the length from tip of nose to be roughly one-third the total length from nose to back of skull.

EYES
Dark. Medium sized eyes to be frontally placed, not large or full, or small and sunk. No white showing at base or top of eye.

EARS
Pendant, heavily feathered. Dark tips an asset.

MOUTH
Upper incisors should close just inside the lower, i.e., a reverse scissor bite. Incisors should be nearly in a straight line. Full dentition is desirable.

Great attention is paid to 'Head and Skull' in the Breed Standard of the Lhasa Apso, so it is essential that we, too, pay great attention to this aspect.

The word "heavy" relating to head furnishings was deleted in the January 2009 revision to the Breed Standard, a decision that was come to by the Kennel Club and is by no means accepted by all Lhasa Apso breeders, myself included. It is to the current Standard we should all now be breeding and judging, but we should not overlook the fact that in Tibet, the breed's homeland, heavy head furnishings are essential and always have been.

Although not mentioned in the Standard, the Lhasa Apso has incredibly long eyelashes, which prevent the hair from falling into the eyes. This means that in the breed's natural habitat, the headfall forms a veil over the eyes, still allowing the dog to see perfectly well, but shielding the eyes from the bright light of that terrain and the startling whiteness of the snow. "Good whiskers and beard" is self-explanatory.

The skull is to be moderately narrow, so although the head is well coated, there should certainly not be a large, broad skull beneath. The term "falling away behind the eyes" has always been open to misinterpretation. It means that the bone of the eye, running from the outer corner, should not protrude as it would in breeds with a rounder eye and a more domed skull. Indeed, the Lhasa Apso skull could be described as a 'happy medium'; not so flat as that of the Chow Chow, nor so domed and 'apple headed' as breeds like the King Charles Spaniel and Chihuahua.

The foreface is straight, meaning it should not be upturned like some other Oriental breeds; the uppermost tip should be in line with the lower eye rim. If the foreface is at the correct angle, the 'stop', which is the indentation between the eyes,

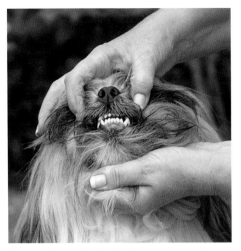

The Breed Standard calls for a reverse scissor bite where the upper incisors close just inside the lower.

will usually conform to the Standard and be 'medium'.

The Breed Standard is specific about the length of the muzzle and the fact that it should not be square. It also quite clearly provides proportions as to the length of the muzzle in relation to the distance from nose to back of skull. "Back" refers to the occiput, which is the bony protuberance that can be easily felt at the back.

To keep the Lhasa Apso's medium length of foreface is not an easy thing to do, for nature will always strive to revert to the norm. We shall come to mouths shortly, but it is because of this that incorrect bites appear from time to time.

The nose is to be black. Occasionally we find Lhasa Apsos with rather weak pigment, sometimes just in the cold season when it is called 'winter nose',

sometimes permanently. This is not, however, correct; an Apso's nose should definitely be black. It is worth mentioning here that the blackness of the nose should be natural and not 'doctored'; to alter it artificially is not only a Kennel Club sin, but also a sin against the breed, and frowned on by those of us judges who will not allow the wool to be pulled over our eyes.

Eyes are dark and should be so, whatever the coat colour. The depth of colour in the Apso's eye adds to that lovely Oriental expression that so becomes the breed. In dogs with light eyes, this typical expression is completely lost. If the head shape is correct, the eye shape, too, will meet the requirements of the Breed Standard: a medium-sized, oval eye that is frontally placed. In an incorrectly round eye, white shows all around it, so the fact that no white is called for at the base or top is necessary if the eye is to be of the required oval shape.

The Lhasa Apso's pendant ear should be moderately low set, for if it is set too high the ear would have some lift to it so the ears would stand slightly off from the skull. This section of the Breed Standard is extremely concise but it actually tells readers quite a lot, also mentioning that the ears are to be well feathered.

The Breed Standard is very specific about the formation of the mouth, which in the English

The neck is strong and should be well arched. The topline is level.

and FCI Standards should be a reverse scissor bite. This means that the upper incisors close just inside the lower. In an ideal mouth, the teeth should be evenly placed with the back of the teeth in the front lower jaw just touching the front of the corresponding upper teeth. Too great a gap and the mouth will be undershot and, of course, the reverse can also happen. In its effort to return to the norm, several Apso mouths end up as level (edge to edge) or normal scissor bites, and can occasionally even be overshot.

In the US Standard the wording is different, saying the preferred bite is either level or slightly undershot. Also, there is no mention of full dentition being desirable. This, in my opinion, is a serious omission, for if the breed were allowed to revert to the problems of earlier years, when two or even three missing incisors occurred frequently, the jaw shape would change accordingly and would become too narrow.

In the English and FCI Standards full dentition is desirable, which ties in with the requirement that the teeth should be in as broad and straight a line as possible, for it is in narrow jaws that you often find missing teeth. A Lhasa Apso should have the normal complement of 42 teeth, 20 in the upper jaw and 22 in the lower; there should be six in each of the upper and lower jaws, set between the canine teeth.

UK
NECK
Strong and well arched.

FOREQUARTERS
Shoulders well laid back. Forelegs straight, heavily furnished with hair.

BODY
Length from point of shoulders to point of buttocks greater than height at withers. Ribs extending well back. Level topline. Strong loin. Balanced and compact.

In a trimmed Apso, it is easier to see the straight forelegs that are required by the Standard.

HINDQUARTERS
Well developed with good muscle. Good angulation. Heavily furnished with hair. Hocks when viewed from behind parallel and not too close together.

FEET
Round, cat-like with firm pads. Well feathered.

USA

BODY SHAPE
The length from point of shoulders to point of buttocks longer than height at withers, well ribbed up, strong loin, well-developed quarters and thighs.

LEGS
Forelegs straight; both forelegs and hind legs heavily furnished with hair.

FEET
Well feathered, should be round and catlike, with good pads.

FCI

NECK
Strong, well covered with a dense mane which is more pronounced in dogs than in bitches.

FOREQUARTERS
Shoulders should be well laid back. Forelegs straight, heavily furnished with hair.

BODY
The length from point of shoulders to point of buttocks greater than height at withers. Well ribbed up. Level top-line. Strong loin. Well balanced and compact.

HINDQUARTERS
Well developed with good muscle. Good angulation. Heavily furnished. The hocks when viewed from behind should be parallel and not too close together.

FEET
Round and cat-like, with good pads. Well-feathered.

An Apso's neck is strong and well

arched, but the Standard does not call for a long neck, so we are not aiming for over-long or 'swan' necks.

Shoulders should be well laid back, indicating a reasonable slope backwards to the withers. Because the blades actually angle inward, there is only a fairly narrow gap between the uppermost points of the scapulae, at the withers. Sadly, there are many Apsos with shoulders that are too upright, not allowing them to achieve the free movement that is so desired in this breed.

The forelegs should be straight, but it is extremely difficult to breed for legs that are absolutely straight if we are to keep height, rib shape and shoulder placement typical of the breed. Nonetheless that is what we must aim for, though we are certainly not looking for fronts that would more befit a terrier. A noticeable bow must be avoided at all costs, as should an 'east-west' front, in which the toes point outward. As in so many breeds, several Apsos have a tendency to be 'out at elbow' or loose in the elbow joint, which, again, is something we should strive to avoid.

The length from point of shoulders to point of buttocks is

The hindquarters should be well developed with good muscle.

to be greater than the height at withers, though the Standard gives us no indication of in what proportion. Clearly we are not looking for a square dog, as is the Tibetan Terrier, but neither should we be looking for a dog that is excessively long. When judging this breed, which is relatively low to the ground, grass, especially if it is long, can play many a trick on the eyes, which is why a judge's assessment of this breed is so important on the table where the

complete outline can be seen.

In its natural habitat of Tibet, plenty of heart and lung room were essential if the breed were to thrive, so unless we forget about the breed's roots, which we should never do, the shape of the ribcage is extremely important. The ribs are well sprung, but neither barrelled nor slab-sided, and they should extend a good way back, for they need to be capacious. In depth they should reach virtually to the elbow joint. Correct ribbing is another area in which many representatives of the breed fail, the loins being too long and the ribcage being too short. Such Apsos would simply not survive in their homeland, it's as simple as that!

The Lhasa Apso Breed Standard requires the topline to be level, so it should neither dip nor roach, either whilst standing or whilst on the move. A poor topline often results from the imbalance of the forequarters compared to the hind construction, usually sloping upwards to the hindquarters rather than the other way around. Sometimes the bones of the hind legs are too long compared with those in the front, and to correct this fault many a show dog is over-stretched behind in an endeavour to conceal it.

Another reason for a poor topline is that the hindquarters are too straight in stifle, and yet another is that the loin is weak, resulting in the topline moving up and down like a wave when the dog is in motion. So we can see clearly how all parts of the Breed Standard interact with one another. The Lhasa Apso is to be balanced and compact, so exaggeration is not required in any department; this we should all strive to remember.

Regarding 'Hindquarters' the Standard asks for good angulation, but it should not be excessive. If the hind angulation is too great, this will affect movement, for the hind legs will be capable of covering more ground than the forelegs. The dog will therefore have to find some way of compensating, most probably by throwing up the feet behind and showing the whole pad, which is incorrect for the breed. A Lhasa Apso should show a little of his pad as he moves away, but no more than about a third. The Standard also requires good muscle, so exercise of the correct kind must be given and this should not just consist of bouncing up and down in a soft-bottomed crate, which so very sadly happens on occasion in some countries.

Hocks should be parallel and not too close together when viewed from behind. This means that clearly 'cow hocks' and 'sickle hocks' are not in keeping with the Standard. Another fault in hindquarter construction to be

The tail is set on high and carried over the back. *© Carol Ann Johnson*

guarded against is the hocks beings too close together; this is generally coupled with narrow hind construction, which, in turn, can bring with it whelping problems.

An Apso's feet should be cat-like, meaning that they are similar in overall shape to those of a cat, but each digit has rather less flexibility of movement, as each individual pad is closer together. But although less flexible than the feet of a cat, there is indeed gripping power in a Lhasa Apso's foot. This is necessary in the breed's homeland and explains why some Apsos are perfectly capable of climbing vertical fencing panels! The feet are to be well feathered, meaning that the coat grows completely over them, necessitating careful trimming, including between the pads.

UK
TAIL
High-set, carried well over back but not like a pot-hook. Often a kink at end. Well feathered.

USA
TAIL AND CARRIAGE
Well feathered, should be carried well over back in a screw; there may be a kink at the end. A low carriage of stern is a serious fault.

FCI
TAIL
High set, carried well over back and not like a pot-hook. There is often a kink at the end. Well feathered.

The tail of the Lhasa Apso is set high enough that it feels comfortable with its tail up at all

ON THE MOVE

Movement should be free and jaunty.

When viewed from the rear, the Apso should show only a little pad when he is on the move.

times. Even when a puppy is still in the nest it is easy to pick out those with really good tail sets. They will keep their tails up whilst eating, whereas those with slightly less good sets will probably drop them while concentrating on their food. This does not imply that the latter have poor tail sets, just that they are more likely to drop them from time to time.

If a tail is set sufficiently high, it will be carried naturally over the back while standing and while moving, but it should not be looped over in the manner of a shepherd's crook, termed 'pot hook'. Obviously, an Apso that is

nervous or lacks confidence in the ring may drop its tail, but this does not necessarily mean that its tail is low set.

The Standard says there may be a kink at the end; this is a trait that is rapidly being lost these days and is not something that a judge will fault if not present. The kink is a tiny bend, about 12mm (half an inch) or so from the end of the tail, and one must never try to straighten it out or it may break for it is so firmly bent!

UK
GAIT/MOVEMENT
Free and jaunty.

FCI
Free and jaunty

The Breed Standard merely asks for 'free and jaunty', which gives little detail and can be open to misinterpretation. Free implies a certain fluidity of stride, unrestricted and not stilted as, for example, in some of the terrier breeds. As mentioned earlier, some Apsos have shoulders that are too upright, thus producing the same terrier-like movement that is uncharacteristic of the Lhasa Apso. The very fact that the Apso is longer than it is high

The topcoat is long and straight, and is hard in texture.

gives it a facility for freedom of movement. The Apso should move true and to do this the elbows should be tightly placed against the side of the ribcage; elbows should not be out, nor indeed should they be tied, for both will give rise to incorrect movement. If the elbows are out, the more common of the two faults, the front legs will tend to plait and weave when they move; if tied, the front legs will have a tendency to be thrown out. Both these faults in movement can be seen clearly by a careful judge's eye, despite the long flowing coat.

'Jaunty' is an unusual adjective to use in relation to a dog's movement and can so often be used as an excuse for poor movement in which an Apso bobs up and down or rolls from side to side when moving. Jaunty literally means that the dog shows that it is cheerful, confident and generally pleased with life.

UK
COAT
Top coat long, heavy, straight, hard neither woolly nor silky. Moderate undercoat. Coat never impeding action.

USA
COAT
Heavy, straight, hard, not woolly nor silky, of good length, and very dense.

FCI
COAT
Top coat heavy, straight and hard, not woolly or silky, of good length. Dense under-coat.

The Lhasa Apso has a double coat, comprising a top coat, which is long, heavy, straight and hard, and an undercoat which in the UK until the mid-1980s also read "dense", but was then

123

A full coat with furnishings only comes with maturity.

changed to read "moderate". Personally, I still feel the former is the more correct, as it is the undercoat that gives this breed the much-needed insulation to live in the extreme climatic conditions of Tibet; it gives protection both against the heat and the bitter cold. However, the change was brought in because it was considered that when presenting our dogs for the show ring, much of the undercoat is groomed out anyway, which indeed is true. It is the undercoat that forms the mats beneath the top coat, and, if not removed, the dog would become very heavily matted. Nevertheless, I would urge breeders never to try to breed out undercoat, for this is

characteristic of the breed and without it an Apso would simply not be an Apso any longer!

The top coat should not be woolly or silky, and it should be noted that it is to be hard, not harsh, for the latter would easily break off at the ends, which an Apso's coat should not. Each strand of hair is strong and carries a certain amount of natural oil, which adds to the weight of the topcoat.

The Lhasa Apso's coat is unlike most other canine coats and was spun to make clothing in the Himalaya, where absolutely everything is put to good use.

In the Breed Standard there are numerous references to coat

furnishings and when taken in isolation these do indeed relate to the areas of the dog on which the coat seems to grow in natural profusion. Typically a Lhasa Apso is a slow-maturing breed, so the full furnishings may not appear until well into adulthood.

UK
COLOUR
Golden, sandy, honey, dark grizzle, slate, smoke, parti-colour, black, white or brown. All equally acceptable

USA
COLOR
All colors equally acceptable with or without dark tips to ears and beard.

In Tibet, it is not unusual to see liver coloured dogs.
© *Juliette Cunliffe*

FCI
COLOURS
Golden, sandy, honey, dark grizzle, slate, smoke, parti-colour, black, white or brown.

According to the Breed Standard, all colours listed are equally acceptable, but as colour descriptions can be open to interpretation, we should keep in mind that because the Standard also calls for a black nose, liver and chocolate-coloured Apsos, which genetically have similarly coloured noses, are not acceptable. It may, however, be worth noting that in Tibet and other parts of the Himalaya there are many chocolate and liver Lhasa Apsos, and these are most

certainly not thought of badly.

All listed colours are held in equal esteem. Certainly, in the past there have been colour preferences, but these were due to erroneous beliefs, so today this is no longer an issue. I do, however, feel that as the wording 'black tips an asset' in relation to the ears was written out of the UK Standard in the 1980s we must guard against losing pigment, because some coats now carry no black at all. It is always sensible to incorporate into a breeding programme dogs that are either black or carry some black in their coat so as not to increase the incidence of lack of pigment, which, generations down the line, will be exceedingly difficult to re-

generate. Undoubtedly, to see a line of Lhasa Apsos with coats of many hues is a sight to behold; all the better if all of them have black noses!

UK
SIZE
Ideal height: dogs: 25cms (10 ins) at shoulders; bitches slightly smaller.

USA
SIZE
Variable, but about 10 inches or 11 inches at shoulder for dogs, bitches slightly smaller.

FCI
Size: Ideal height: 25.4 cm (10 in) at shoulder for dogs; bitches slightly smaller.

It is the judge's job to find the dog which most closely resembles the word picture outlined in the Breed Standard.

little more height. This has had an inevitable bearing on the height of Lhasa Apsos also in Britain today, but we should all be striving for the ideal.

UK
FAULTS
Any departure from the foregoing points should be considered a fault and the seriousness with which the fault should be regarded should be in exact proportion to its degree and its effect upon the health and welfare of the dog. Note: Male animals should have two apparently normal testicles fully descended into the scrotum.

FCI
Note: Male animals should have two apparently normal testicles fully descended into the scrotum.

Although at first glance the Standard regarding size looks straightforward, there is a little more to it than meets the eye. The ideal height for dogs is 25cms (10 ins) at shoulders, but the word 'ideal' gives rise to certain variations, though these should never be too great. In the show rings these days, few dogs are the ideal height as per the Standard; most are larger. But if a dog were even half an inch below the ideal it would appear very small, even though it may be nearer to the ideal than the much larger dogs in the ring. Bitches should be slightly smaller than dogs, but in view of the current disparity of size within the breed, some bitches are actually larger than males.

It is relevant to bear in mind that the American Standard is worded differently: "Variable, but about 10 inches or 11 inches at shoulder for dogs, bitches slightly smaller", thereby allowing for a little more height.

In no British Breed Standard are faults any longer listed individually, as they used to be decades ago, but instead all deviations from the Standards are considered a fault, and the seriousness with which they should be regarded is to be in proportion not only to its degree but now also its effect upon the health and welfare of the dog.

All males should have two apparently normal testicles fully descended into the scrotum, and, if this is not the case, exhibitors should be able to provide the judge with a veterinary letter explaining that an operation has taken place, and why.

SUMMING UP

So, the Lhasa Apso Breed Standard gives a pretty clear outline of the breed, but reading a Standard alone is not sufficient to enable an enthusiast, future breeder or judge to understand the breed fully. It is essential to 'talk Apso' with as many knowledgeable people as you can and to go along to any seminars that are on offer for the breed, even if it means travelling some distance and perhaps foregoing a show or two.

You will pick up some unwritten characteristics that are specific to the Lhasa Apso, such as the need for a 'chin' to give that lovely Tibetan expression that is so desirable. The chin does not feature in the Standard, but comes about because of the placement of the lower jaw. However, even though the bite may be correct, it is possible for a Lhasa Apso to be lacking in chin, and this alters the expression.

So although the written word is important and the Breed Standard must be adhered to, if you want to really understand the Lhasa Apso, you must explore every opportunity to learn more. When you have done so, only then can you fully appreciate this wonderful breed that has captured your heart and will hopefully continue to do so for many years to come.

With a breed such as the Lhasa Apso there is always something new to learn, and when you have learned well, you too, may perhaps have a successful Champion like this one. For comparison's sake, this is the same dog that was clipped off after his show career was over and can be seen in the grooming photos in Chapter 5. © Carol Ann Johnson

HAPPY AND HEALTHY

Chapter 8

L hasa Apsos are real characters with a life span that can run well into double figures. The Lhasa Apso is renowned as a faithful companion and a willing friend on a non-conditional basis. He will, however, of necessity rely on you for food and shelter, accident prevention and medication. A healthy Lhasa Apso is a happy chap, looking to please and amuse his owner.

There are only a few genetic conditions recognised in the Lhasa Apso, which will be covered in depth later in the chapter.

ROUTINE HEALTH CARE

VACCINATION
There is much debate over the issue of vaccination at the moment. The timing of the final part of the initial vaccination course for a puppy and the frequency of subsequent booster vaccinations are both under scrutiny. An evaluation of the relative risk for each disease plays a part, depending on the local situation.

Many owners think that the actual vaccination is the protection, so that their puppy can go out for walks as soon as he or she has had the final part of the puppy vaccination course. This is not the case. The rationale behind vaccination is to stimulate the immune system into producing protective antibodies, which will be triggered if the patient is subsequently exposed to that particular disease. This means that a further one or two weeks will have to pass before an effective level of protection will have developed.

Vaccines against viruses stimulate longer-lasting protection than those against bacteria, whose effect may only persist for a matter of months in some cases. There is also the possibility of an individual failing to mount a full immune response to a vaccination: although the vaccine schedule may have been followed as recommended, that particular dog remains vulnerable.

A dog's level of protection against rabies, as demonstrated by the antibody titre in a blood sample, is routinely tested in the UK in order to fulfil the requirements of the Pet Travel Scheme (PETS). This is not required at the current time with any other individual diseases in order to gauge the need for booster vaccination or to determine the effect of a course of vaccines; instead, your veterinary surgeon will advise a protocol based upon the vaccines available, local disease prevalence, and the lifestyle of you and your dog.

The booster provides an opportunity to give your dog an annual check up.
© *Juliette Cunliffe*

It is worth remembering that maintaining a fully effective level of immune protection against the disease appropriate to your locale is vital: these are serious diseases, which may result in the death of your dog, and some may have the potential to be passed on to his human family (so-called zoonotic potential for transmission). This is where you will be grateful for your veterinary surgeon's own knowledge and advice.

The American Animal Hospital Association laid down guidance at the end of 2006 for the vaccination of dogs in North America. Core diseases were defined as distemper, adenovirus, parvovirus and rabies. So-called non-core diseases are kennel cough, Lyme disease and leptospirosis. A decision to vaccinate against one or more non-core diseases will be based on an individual's level of risk, determined on lifestyle and where you live in the US.

Do remember, however, that the booster visit to the veterinary surgery is not 'just' for a booster. I am regularly correcting my clients when they announce that they have 'just' brought their pet for a booster. Instead, this appointment is a chance for a full health check and evaluation of how a particular dog is doing. After all, we are all conversant with the adage that a human year is equivalent to seven canine years.

There have been attempts in recent times to reset the scale for two reasons: small breeds live longer than giant breeds, and dogs are living longer than previously. I have seen dogs of 17 and 18 years of age, but to say a dog is 119 or 126 years old is plainly meaningless. It does emphasise the fact, though, that a dog's health can change dramatically over the course of a single year, because dogs age at a far faster rate than humans.

For me as a veterinary surgeon, the booster vaccination visit is a challenge: how much can I find of which the owner was unaware, such as rotten teeth or a heart murmur? Even monitoring bodyweight year upon year is of use, because a dog's weight can creep up, or down, without an owner realising. Being overweight is unhealthy, but it may take an outsider's remark to make an owner realise that there is a problem. Conversely, a drop in bodyweight may be the only pointer to an underlying problem.

The diseases against which dogs are vaccinated include:

ADENOVIRUS
Canine adenovirus 1 (CAV-1) affects the liver (hepatitis) and is seen within affected dogs as the classic 'blue eye', while CAV-2 is a cause of kennel cough (see later). Vaccines often include both canine adenoviruses.

DISTEMPER
This disease is sometimes called 'hardpad' from the characteristic changes to the pads of the paws. It has a worldwide distribution, but fortunately vaccination has been very effective at reducing its occurrence. It is caused by a virus and affects the respiratory, gastro-intestinal (gut) and nervous systems, so it causes a wide range of illnesses. Fox and urban stray dog populations are most at risk and are usually responsible for local outbreaks.

KENNEL COUGH
Also known as infectious tracheobronchitis, *Bordetella bronchiseptica* is not only a major cause of kennel cough but also a common secondary infection on top of another cause. Being a bacterium, it is susceptible to treatment with appropriate antibiotics, but the immunity stimulated by the vaccine is therefore short-lived (six to 12 months).

This vaccine is often in a form to be administered down the nostrils in order to stimulate local immunity at the point of entry, so to speak. Do not be alarmed to

Kennel cough is highly contagious and will spread rapidly among dogs that live together.

see your veterinary surgeon using a needle and syringe to draw up the vaccine, because the needle will be replaced with a special plastic introducer, allowing the vaccine to be gently instilled into each nostril. Dogs generally resent being held more than the actual intra-nasal vaccine, and I have learnt that covering the patient's eyes helps greatly.

Kennel cough is, however, rather a catch-all term for any cough spreading within a dog population – not just in kennels, but also between dogs at a training session or breed show, or even mixing in the park. Many of these infections may not be *B. bronchiseptica* but other viruses,

for which one can only treat symptomatically. Parainfluenza virus is often included in a vaccine programme, as it is a common viral cause of kennel cough.

Kennel cough can seem alarming. There is a persistent cough accompanied by the production of white frothy spittle, which can last for a matter of weeks; during this time the patient is highly infectious to other dogs. I remember when it ran through our five Border Collies – there were white patches of froth on the floor wherever you looked! Other features include sneezing, a runny nose, and eyes sore with conjunctivitis. Fortunately, these infections are generally self-limiting, most dogs recovering without any long-lasting problems, but an elderly dog may be knocked sideways by it, akin to the effects of a common cold on a frail, elderly person.

LEPTOSPIROSIS

This disease is caused by *Leptospira interogans*, a spiral-shaped bacterium. There are several natural variants or serovars. Each is characteristically found in one or more particular host animal species, which then acts as a reservoir, intermittently shedding leptospires in the urine. Infection can also be picked up at mating, via bite wounds, across the placenta, or through eating the carcases of infected animals (such as rats).

A serovar will cause actual clinical disease in an individual when two conditions are fulfilled: the individual is not the natural host species, and is also not immune to that particular serovar.

Leptospirosis is a zoonotic disease, known as Weil's disease in humans, with implications for all those in contact with an affected dog. It is also commonly called rat jaundice, reflecting the rat's important role as a carrier. The UK National Rodent Survey 2003 found a wild brown rat population of 60 million, equivalent at the time to one rat per person. Wherever you live in the UK, rats are endemic, which means that there is as much a risk to the Lhasa Apso living with a family in a town as the Lhasa Apso leading a rural lifestyle.

Signs of illness reflect the organs affected by a particular serovar. In humans, there may be a flu-like illness or a more serious, often life-threatening disorder involving major body organs. The illness in a susceptible dog may be mild, the dog recovering within two to three weeks without treatment but going on to develop long-term liver or kidney disease. In contrast, peracute illness may result in a rapid deterioration and death following an initial malaise and fever. There may also be anorexia, vomiting, diarrhoea, abdominal pain, joint pain, increased thirst and urination rate, jaundice, and ocular changes. Haemorrhage is also a common feature, manifesting as bleeding under the skin, nosebleeds, and the presence of blood in the urine and faeces.

Treatment requires rigorous intravenous fluid therapy to support the kidneys. Being a bacterial infection, it is possible to treat leptospirosis with specific antibiotics, although a prolonged course of several weeks is needed. Strict hygiene and barrier nursing are required in order to avoid onward transmission of the disease.

Vaccination reduces the severity of disease, but cannot prevent the dog becoming a carrier.

The situation in America is less clear-cut. Blanket vaccination against leptospirosis is not considered necessary, because it only occurs in certain areas. There has also been a shift in the serovars implicated in clinical disease, reflecting the effectiveness of vaccination and the migration of wildlife reservoirs carrying different serovars from rural areas, so you

Lyme disease is still relatively rare in the UK.
© Carol Ann Johnson

must be guided by your veterinarian's knowledge of the local situation.

LYME DISEASE

This is a bacterial infection transmitted by hard ticks. It is restricted to those specific areas of the US where ticks are found.

Clinical disease is manifested primarily as limping due to arthritis, but other organs affected include the heart, kidneys and nervous system. It is readily treatable with appropriate antibiotics, once diagnosed, but the causal bacterium, *Borrelia burgdorferi*, is not cleared from the body totally and will persist.

Prevention requires both vaccination and tick control, especially as there are other diseases transmitted by ticks. Ticks carrying *B. burgdorferi* will transmit it to humans as well, but an infected dog cannot pass it to a human.

PARVOVIRUS (CPV)

Canine parvovirus disease first appeared in the late 1970s, when it was feared that the UK's dog population would be decimated by it because of the lack of immunity in the general canine population. While this was a terrifying possibility at the time, fortunately it did not happen.

There are two forms of the virus (CPV-1, CPV-2) affecting domesticated dogs. It is highly contagious, picked up via the mouth/nose from infected faeces. The incubation period is about five days. CPV-2 causes two types of illness: gastro-enteritis and

RABIES

This is another zoonotic disease and there are very strict control measures in place. Vaccines were once available in the UK only on an individual basis for dogs being taken abroad. Pets travelling into the UK had to serve six months' compulsory quarantine so that any pet incubating rabies would be identified before release back into the general population. Under the Pet Travel Scheme (PETS), provided certain criteria are met (check the DEFRA website for up-to-date information) then dogs can re-enter the UK without being quarantined.

Dogs to be imported into the US have to show that they were vaccinated against rabies at least 30 days previously; otherwise, they have to serve effective internal quarantine for 30 days from the date of vaccination against rabies, in order to ensure they are not incubating rabies. The exception is dogs entering from countries recognised as being rabies-free, in which case it has to be proved that they lived in that country for at least six months beforehand.

heart disease in puppies born to unvaccinated dams, both of which often result in death. Infection of puppies under three weeks of age with CPV-1 manifests as diarrhoea, vomiting, difficulty breathing, and fading puppy syndrome. CPV-1 can cause abortion and foetal abnormalities in breeding bitches.

Occurrence is mainly low now, thanks to vaccination, although a recent outbreak in my area did claim the lives of several puppies and dogs. It is also occasionally seen in the elderly unvaccinated dog.

PARASITES

A parasite is defined as an organism deriving benefit on a one-way basis from another, the

host. It goes without saying that it is not to the parasite's advantage to harm the host to such an extent that the benefit is lost, especially if it results in the death of the host. This means a dog could harbour parasites, internal and/or external, without there being any signs apparent to the owner. Many canine parasites can, however, transfer to humans with variable consequences, so routine preventative treatment is advised against particular parasites.

Just as with vaccination, risk assessment plays a part – for example, there is no need for routine heartworm treatment in the UK (at present), but it is vital in the US and in Mediterranean countries.

Puppies should be routinely treated for roundworm.

ROUNDWORMS (NEMATODES)

These are the spaghetti-like worms that you may have seen passed in faeces or brought up in vomit. Most of the deworming treatments in use today cause the adult roundworms to disintegrate, thankfully, so that treating puppies in particular is not as unpleasant as it used to be!

Most puppies will have a worm burden, mainly of a particular roundworm species (*Toxocara canis*), which reactivates within the dam's tissues during pregnancy and passes to the foetuses developing in the womb. It is therefore important to treat the dam both during and after pregnancy, as well as the puppies.

Professional advice is to continue worming every one to three months. There are roundworm eggs in the environment and, unless you examine your dog's faeces under a microscope on a very regular basis for the presence of roundworm eggs, you will be unaware of your dog having picked up roundworms, unless he should have such a heavy burden that he passes the adults.

It takes a few weeks from the time that a dog swallows a *Toxocara canis* roundworm egg to himself passing viable eggs (the pre-patent period). These eggs are not immediately infective to other animals, requiring a period of maturation in the environment, which is primarily temperature-

dependent and therefore shorter in the summer (as little as two weeks) than in the winter. The eggs can survive in the environment for two years and more.

There are deworming products that are active all the time, which will provide continuous protection when administered as often as directed. Otherwise, treating every month will, in effect, cut in before a dog could theoretically become a source of roundworm eggs to the general population.

It is the risk to human health that is so important: *T. canis* roundworms will migrate within our tissues and cause all manner of problems, not least of which (but fortunately rarely) is

HEARTWORM (DIROFILARIA IMMITIS)

Heartworm infection has been diagnosed in dogs all over the world. There are two prerequisites: the presence of mosquitoes, and a warm, humid climate.

When a female mosquito bites an infected animal, it acquires *D. immitis* in its circulating form, as microfilariae. A warm environmental temperature is needed for these microfilariae to develop into the infective third-stage larvae (L3) within the mosquitoes, the so-called intermediate host. L3 larvae are then transmitted by the mosquito when it next bites a dog. Therefore, while heartworm infection is found in all parts of the United States, it is at differing levels. An occurrence in Alaska, for example, is probably a reflection of a visiting dog having previously picked up the infection elsewhere.

Heartworm infection is not currently a problem in the UK, except for those dogs contracting it while abroad without suitable preventative treatment. Global warming and its effect on the UK's climate, however, could change that.

It is a potentially life-threatening condition, with dogs of all breeds and ages being susceptible without preventative treatment. The larvae can grow to 14 inches within the right side of the heart, causing primarily signs of heart failure and ultimately liver and kidney damage. It can be treated but prevention is a better plan. In the US, regular blood tests for the presence of infection are advised, coupled with appropriate preventative measures, so I would advise liaison with your veterinary surgeon.

For dogs travelling to heartworm-endemic areas of the EU, such as the Mediterranean coast, preventative treatment should be started before leaving the UK and maintained during the visit. Again, this is best arranged with your veterinary surgeon.

blindness. If a dog has roundworms, the eggs also find their way on to his coat where they can be picked up during stroking. Sensible hygiene is therefore important. You should always carefully pick up your dog's faeces and dispose of them appropriately, thereby preventing the maturation of any eggs present in the fresh faeces.

TAPEWORMS (CESTODES)
When considering the general dog population, the primary source of the commonest tapeworm species will be fleas, which can carry the eggs. Most multi-wormers will be active against these tapeworms. They are not a threat to human health, but it is unpleasant to see the wriggly ricegrain tapeworm segments emerging from your dog's back passage while he is lying in front of the fire, and usually when you have guests for dinner!

A tapeworm of significance to human health is *Echinococcus granulosus*, found in a few parts of the UK, mainly in Wales. Man is an intermediate host for this tapeworm, along with sheep, cattle and pigs. Inadvertent ingestion of eggs passed in the faeces of an infected dog is followed by the development of so-called hydatid cysts in major organs, such as the lungs and liver, necessitating surgical removal. Dogs become infected through eating raw meat containing hydatid cysts. Cooking will kill hydatid cysts, so avoid feeding raw meat and offal in areas of high risk.

There are specific requirements

for treatment with praziquantel within 24 to 48 hours of return into the UK under the PETS. This is to prevent the inadvertent introduction of *Echinococcus multilocularis*, a tapeworm carried by foxes on mainland Europe, which is transmissible to humans, causing serious or even fatal liver disease.

FLEAS

There are several species of flea, which are not host-specific. A dog can be carrying cat and human fleas as well as dog fleas, but the same flea treatment will kill and/or control them all. It is also accepted that environmental control is a vital part of a flea control programme. This is because the adult flea is only on the animal for as long as it takes to have a blood meal and to breed; the remainder of the life cycle occurs in the house, car, caravan, shed…

There is a vast array of flea control products available, with various routes of administration: collar, powder, spray, 'spot-on', or oral. Flea control needs to be applied to all pets in the house, regardless of whether they leave the house, since fleas can be introduced into the home by other pets and their human owners. Discuss your specific flea control needs with your veterinary surgeon.

Spot-on treatment is effective in preventing infestation from fleas.

MITES

There are five types of mite that can affect dogs:

i)Demodex canis: This mite is a normal inhabitant of canine hair follicles, passed from the bitch to her pups as they suckle. The development of actual skin disease or demodicosis depends on the individual. It is seen frequently around the time of puberty and after a bitch's first season, associated with hormonal changes. There may, however, be an inherited weakness in an individual's immune system, enabling multiplication of the mite.

The localised form consists of areas of fur loss without itchiness, generally around the face and on the forelimbs, and 90 per cent will recover without treatment. The other 10 per cent develop the juvenile-onset generalised form, of which half will recover spontaneously. The other half may be depressed, go off their food, and show signs of itchiness due to secondary bacterial skin infections.

Treatment is often prolonged over several months and consists of regular bathing with a specific miticidal shampoo, often clipping away fur to improve access to the skin, together with a suitable antibiotic by mouth. There is also now a licensed 'spot-on' preparation available. Progress is monitored by the examination of deep skin scrapings for the presence of the mite; the initial diagnosis is based upon abnormally high numbers of the mite, often with live individuals being seen.

Some Lhasa Apsos may develop demodicosis for the first time in middle-age (more than four years of age). This often reflects underlying immunosuppression by an internal disease, so it is important to identify such a cause and correct it where possible, as well as treating the skin condition.

(ii) Sarcoptes scabei: This characteristically causes an intense pruritus or itchiness in the affected Lhasa Apso, causing him to incessantly scratch and bite at himself, leading to marked fur loss and skin trauma. Initially starting on the elbows, earflaps and hocks, without treatment the skin on the rest of the body can become affected, with thickening and pigmentation of the skin. Secondary bacterial infections are common.

Unlike *Demodex*, this mite lives at the skin surface, and it can be hard to find in skin scrapings. It is therefore not unusual to treat a patient for sarcoptic mange (scabies) based on the appearance of the problem even with negative skin scraping findings, and especially if there is a history of contact with foxes, which are a frequent source of the scabies mite.

It will spread between dogs and can therefore also be found in situations where large numbers of dogs from different backgrounds are mixing together. It will cause itchiness in human, although the mite cannot complete its life cycle on us, so treating all affected dogs should be sufficient. Fortunately, there is now a highly effective 'spot-on' treatment for *Sarcoptes scabei*.

(iii) Cheyletiella yasguri: This is the fur mite most commonly found on dogs. It is often called 'walking dandruff' because it can be possible to see collections of the small white mite moving about over the skin surface. There is excessive scale and dandruff

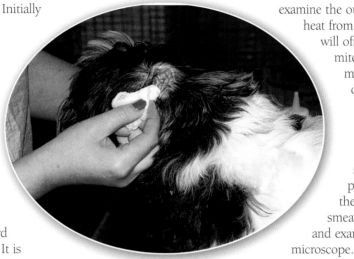

Ears must be checked regularly as the build up of wax could indicate the presence of ear mites.

© *Juliette Cunliffe*

formation, and mild itchiness. It is be transmissible to humans, causing a pruritic rash.

Diagnosis is by microscopic examination of skin scrapings, coat combings and sticky tape impressions from the skin and fur. Treatment is with an appropriate insecticide, as advised by your veterinary surgeon.

(iv) Otodectes cynotis: A highly transmissible otitis externa (outer ear infection) results from the presence in the outer ear canal of this ear mite characterised by exuberant production of dark earwax. The patient will frequently shake his head and rub at the ear(s) affected. The mites can also spread on to the skin adjacent to the opening of the external ear canal, and may transfer elsewhere, such as to the paws.

When using an otoscope to

examine the outer ear canal, the heat from the light source will often cause any ear mites present to start moving around. I often offer owners the chance to have a look, because it really is quite an extraordinary sight! It is also possible to identify the mite from earwax smeared on to a slide and examined under a microscope.

Cats are a common source of ear mites. It is not unusual to find ear mites during the routine examination of puppies and kittens. Treatment options include specific eardrops acting against both the mite and any secondary infections present in the auditory canal, and certain 'spot-on' formulations. It is vital to treat all dogs and cats in the household to prevent recycling of the mite between individuals.

(v) The free-living mite (Neo-) Trombicula autumnalis or harvest mite: This can cause an intense local irritation on the skin. Its larvae are picked up from undergrowth, so they are characteristically found as a bright orange patch on the web of skin between the digits of the paws. It feeds on skin cells before dropping off to complete its life cycle in the environment.

Its name is a little misleading, because it is not restricted to the autumn nor to harvest-time; I find it on the earflaps of cats from

TICKS

Ticks have become an increasing problem in recent years throughout Britain. Their physical presence causes irritation, but it is their potential to spread disease that causes concern. A tick will transmit any infection previously contracted while feeding on an animal: for example Borrelia burgdorferi, the causal agent of Lyme disease (see page 133).

The life cycle of the tick is curious: each life stage takes a year to develop and move on to the next. Long grass is a major habitat. The vibration of animals moving through the grass will stimulate the larva, nymph or adult to climb up a blade of grass and wave its legs in the air as it 'quests' for a host on to which to latch for its next blood meal. Humans are as likely to be hosts, so ramblers and orienteers are advised to cover their legs when going through rough long grass.

Removing a tick is simple – provided your dog will stay still. The important rule is to twist gently so that the tick is persuaded to let go with its mouthparts. Grasp the body of the tick as near to your dog's skin as possible, either between thumb and fingers or with a specific tick-removing instrument, and then rotate in one direction until the tick comes away. I keep a plastic tick hook in my wallet at all times.

late June onwards, depending on the prevailing weather. It will also bite humans.

Treatment depends on identifying and avoiding hotspots for picking up harvest mites, if possible. Checking the skin, especially the paws, after exercise and mechanically removing any mites found will reduce the chances of irritation, which can be treated symptomatically. Insecticides can also be applied – be guided by your veterinary surgeon.

A-Z OF COMMON AILMENTS

ANAL SACS, IMPACTED
The anal sacs lie on either side of the anus at approximately four and eight o'clock, if compared with the face of a clock. They fill with a particularly pungent fluid, which is emptied on to the faeces as they move past the sacs to exit from the anus. Theories abound as to why these sacs should become impacted periodically and seemingly more so in some dogs than others.

The irritation of impacted anal sacs is often seen as 'scooting', when the backside is dragged along the ground. Some dogs will also gnaw at their back feet or over the rump.

Increasing the fibre content of the diet helps some dogs; in others, there is underlying skin disease. It may be a one-off occurrence for no apparent reason. Sometimes an infection can become established, requiring antibiotic therapy, which may need to be coupled with flushing out the infected sac under sedation or general anaesthesia. More rarely, a dog will present with an apparently acute-onset anal sac abscess, which is incredibly painful.

DIARRHOEA
Cause and treatment much as Gastritis (see below).

EAR INFECTIONS
The dog has a long external ear canal, initially vertical then horizontal, leading to the eardrum, which protects the middle ear. If your Lhasa Apso is shaking his head, then his ears will need to be inspected with an auroscope by a veterinary surgeon in order to identify any cause, and to ensure the eardrum is intact. A sample may be taken from the canal to be examined under the microscope and

A sudden change of diet can cause a stomach upset.
© *Juliette Cunliffe*

cultured, to identify causal agents before prescribing appropriate eardrops containing antibiotic, antifungal agent and/or steroid. Predisposing causes of otitis externa or infection in the external ear canal include:

- Presence of a foreign body, such as a grass awn
- Ear mites, which are intensely irritating to the dog and stimulate the production of brown wax, predisposing to infection
- Previous infections, causing the canal's lining to thicken, narrowing the canal and reducing ventilation
- Swimming – some Lhasa Apsos will swim; water trapped in the external ear canal can lead to infection, especially if the water is not clean. Likewise, care should be taken around the ears when washing and bathing your Lhasa Apso.

FOREIGN BODIES

Internal: Items swallowed in haste without checking whether they will be digested can cause problems if they lodge in the stomach or obstruct the intestines, necessitating surgical removal. Acute vomiting is the main indication. Common objects I have seen removed include stones from the garden, peach stones, babies' dummies, golf balls, and, once, a lady's bra…

It is possible to diagnose a dog with an intestinal obstruction across a waiting room from a particularly 'tucked-up' stance and pained facial expression. These patients bounce back from surgery dramatically. A previously docile and compliant obstructed patient will return for a post-operative check-up and literally bounce into the consulting room.

External: Grass awns are adept at finding their way into orifices such as a nostril, down an ear, and into the soft skin between two digits (toes), whence they start a one-way journey due to the direction of their whiskers. In particular, I remember a grass awn that migrated from a hindpaw, causing abscesses along the way but not yielding itself up until it erupted through the skin in the groin!

GASTRITIS

This is usually a simple stomach upset, most commonly in response to dietary indiscretion. Scavenging constitutes a change in the diet as much as an abrupt switch in the food being fed by the owner. There are also some specific infections causing more severe gastritis/enteritis, which will require treatment from a veterinary surgeon (see also Canine Parvovirus under 'Vaccination' on page ??).

Generally, a day without food, followed by a few days of small, frequent meals of a bland diet (such as cooked chicken or fish), or an appropriate prescription diet, should allow the stomach to settle. It is vital to ensure the patient is drinking and retaining sufficient water to cover losses resulting from the stomach upset in addition to the normal losses to be expected when healthy. Oral rehydration fluid may not be

The Lhasa Apso is an active breed, but watch out for stiffness after exercise as your dog grows older.

very appetising for the patient, in which case cooled boiled water should be offered. Fluids should initially be offered in small but frequent amounts to avoid over-drinking, which can result in further vomiting and thereby dehydration and electrolyte imbalances. It is also important to wean the patient back on to routine food gradually or else another bout of gastritis may occur.

JOINT PROBLEMS

It is not unusual for older Lhasa Apsos to be stiff after exercise, particularly in cold weather. This is not really surprising, given that they are such busy dogs when young. A nine- or 10-year-old Lhasa Apso will not readily forego an extra walk or take kindly to turning for home earlier than usual. Your veterinary surgeon

will be able to advise you on ways of helping your dog cope with stiffness, not least of which will be to ensure that he is not overweight. Arthritic joints do not need to be burdened with extra bodyweight!

LUMPS

Regularly handling and stroking your dog will enable the early detection of lumps and bumps. These may be due to infection (abscess), bruising, multiplication of particular cells from within the body, or even an external parasite (tick). If you are worried about any lump you find, have it checked by a veterinary surgeon.

OBESITY

Being overweight does predispose to many other problems, such as diabetes mellitus, heart disease and joint problems. It is so easily

prevented by simply acting as your Lhasa Apso's conscience. Ignore pleading eyes and feed according to your dog's waistline. The body condition is what matters qualitatively, alongside monitoring that individual's bodyweight as a quantitative measure. The Lhasa Apso should, in my opinion as a health professional, have at least a suggestion of a waist and it should be possible to feel the ribs beneath only a slight layer of fat.

Neutering does not automatically mean that your Lhasa Apso will be overweight. Having an ovario-hysterectomy does slow down the body's rate of working, castration to a lesser extent, but it therefore means that your dog needs less food. I recommend cutting back a little on the amount of food fed a few weeks before neutering to accustom your Lhasa Apso to less food. If she looks a little underweight on the morning of the operation, it will help the veterinary surgeon as well as giving her a little leeway weight-wise afterwards. It is always harder to lose weight after neutering than before, because of this slowing in the body's inherent metabolic rate.

TEETH

Eating food starts with the canine teeth gripping and killing prey in the wild, incisor teeth biting off pieces of food and the molar teeth chewing it. To be able to eat is vital for life, yet the actual health of the teeth is often overlooked: unhealthy teeth can

If you feed a well balanced diet and plan a routine of regular exercise, you will guard against the dangers of obesity.

predispose to disease, and not just by reducing the ability to eat. The presence of infection within the mouth can lead to bacteria entering the bloodstream and then filtering out at major organs, with the potential for serious consequences. That is not to forget that simply having dental pain can affect a dog's wellbeing, as anyone who has had toothache will confirm.

Veterinary dentistry has made huge leaps in recent years, so that it no longer consists of extraction as the treatment of necessity. Good dental health lies in the hands of the owner, starting from the moment the dog comes into your care. Just as we have taken on responsibility for feeding, so we have acquired the task of maintaining good dental and oral hygiene. In an ideal world, we should brush our dogs' teeth as regularly as our own, but the Lhasa Apso puppy who finds having his teeth brushed is a huge game and excuse to roll over and over on the ground requires loads of patience, twice a day.

There are alternative strategies, ranging from dental chewsticks to specially formulated foods, but the main thing is to be aware of your dog's mouth. At least train your puppy to permit full examination of his teeth. This will not only ensure you are checking in his mouth regularly, but will also make your veterinary surgeon's job easier when there is a real need for your dog to 'open wide!'

INHERITED DISORDERS

Any individual, dog or human, may have an inherited disorder by virtue of the genes acquired from the parents. This is significant not only for the health of that individual but also because of the potential for transmitting the disorder on to that individual's offspring and to subsequent generations, depending on the mode of inheritance.

There are control schemes in place for some inherited disorders. In the US, for example, the Canine Eye Registration Foundation (CERF) was set up by dog breeders concerned about heritable eye disease, and provides a database of dogs who have been examined by diplomates of the American College of Veterinary Ophthalmologists.

The Lhasa Apso characteristically has a brachycephalic skull, resulting in a foreshortened nose and shallow orbits (the bony eye sockets). The eyeballs are therefore more prominent and there may be a reduced ability to close the eyelids over them. This, in turn, predisposes to chronic corneal irritation (exposure keratopathy), which, at its most extreme, can lead to ulceration and rupture.

The shape of the Lhasa Apso's head also predisposes to hydrocephalus. There is an abnormal build-up of fluid within the ventricles (cavities) of the brain, exerting unusual pressure on the brain itself. This is a relative common congenital abnormality. Severely affected pups will die shortly after birth, whilst others develop clinical signs before they are three

All breeding stock should be checked for the incidence of inherited conditions.

indications, such as prolonged bleeding when the baby teeth are lost, or unexpected bruising under the skin. A problem may not become apparent until after surgery, such as routine neutering or an injury. Treatment will often require a blood transfusion. Deficient levels of factor IX characterise haemophilia B (Christmas disease). It is a more severe clotting disorder than haemophilia A, and fortunately even more rare.

KERATOCONJUNCTIVITIS SICCA (KCS, dry eye)
Each eye is lubricated by tears produced by two tear glands, one within the eye socket and another smaller one associated with the third eyelid. There appears to be a breed predisposition for KCS, which results when there is inadequate tear production by the glands (hence 'dry eye'), and is usually bilateral, affecting the tear glands in both eyes. It is characterised by a sore, red appearance to the eye with a thick ocular discharge and, ultimately, clouding of the cornea and loss of vision. The cause is generally unknown or inherited. Rarely, dry eye may be as a result of trauma, infection, hypothyroidism or an adverse reaction to a drug.

Diagnosis is made by testing each eye with a Schirmer tear strip, which assesses the tear production. Surgical transposition of the parotid salivary duct was the favoured treatment, but medical therapy is now more often the therapy of choice,

months of age. Mild cases may not be diagnosed until much older.

Signs of hydrocephalus include growth and development falling behind littermates, a pronounced dome to the skull, abnormal movements (such as restless and aimless walking), impaired vision, reduced learning ability (hard to house-train, for example) and seizures.

The Lhasa Apso is a breed where very few inherited conditions have been confirmed to date. In alphabetical order, these include:

CATARACT
A cataract is a cloudiness of the lens of the eye. In the Lhasa Apso, this is the adult-onset form of cataract, occurring in the middle-aged dog (three to six years old), rather than the congenital form seen in other breeds (where some form of lens opacity is present from birth). There is progressive visual impairment. Inheritance is suspected.

ENTROPION
This is an inrolling of the eyelids. Usually the lower eyelids are affected. There are degrees of entropion, ranging from a slight inrolling to the more serious case, requiring surgical correction because of the pain and damage to the surface of the eyeball.

HAEMOPHILIA
Haemophilia is the most common disorder of blood coagulation, inherited in a sex-linked recessive fashion. This means that the male is either affected or clear, whilst females can alternatively be carriers for the trait.

Haemophilia A arises from a deficiency of blood-clotting factor VIII. There are many ways in which haemophilia A can manifest, ranging from a mild bleeding disorder to, at worst, sudden death. There may be early aimed at stimulating the under-active tear glands.

LISSENCEPHALY

This is a rare inherited condition resulting from abnormal development of the nerve cells within the brain before birth. It manifests as seizures, blindness, and abnormal behaviour in puppies shortly after birth. There is no treatment. It can be diagnosed with an MRI scan. The mode of inheritance has not been identified.

PROGRESSIVE RETINAL ATROPHY, GENERALISED (GPRA)

Degeneration of the retina first manifests as night blindness in the young animal. It is a progressive disorder, culminating in total blindness. It is controlled under Schedule A of the BVA/KC/ISDS Scheme in the UK.

* British Veterinary Association/Kennel Club/International Sheepdog Society Scheme

RENAL DYSPLASIA, JUVENILE (JRD)

The glomeruli in the kidneys of affected individuals fail to mature properly, with signs of kidney failure becoming apparent from a few months of age onwards, although some may not show signs until as old as four or five years. Initially, owners notice an increased thirst together with the passing of large volumes of pale (dilute) urine, and a failure to grow and thrive if affected as a puppy. Weight loss, lethargy, vomiting and collapse occur in the later stages.

There may also be concurrent renal glucosuria: the presence of glucose in the urine with a normal blood glucose level (unlike the situation in diabetes mellitus where there is hyperglycaemia, or raised blood glucose).

The ability to concentrate urine can be used as a guide to overall kidney function, but a definitive diagnosis can only really be made by examining a kidney biopsy.

The mode of inheritance is under active investigation, which is close to delivering positive results. It is known to not be sex-linked. Two genes are thought to be involved. Individuals can be carriers without developing the disease, so it is hoped that a DNA test will be available in the near future.

SKIN CONDITIONS

There are a number of skin disorders that may have a hereditary basis, especially where there may be an underlying allergy, which is often seasonal. Effects range from recurrent skin infections to compulsive licking of the paws (apparent as the classic pink discoloration of the fur) and incessant itchiness.

SEBACEOUS ADENITIS

This is is an important skin condition, which may affect any breed of dog (and rarely the cat) with certain breeds, such as the Lhasa Apso, being over-represented.

Sebaceous adenitis (SA) strictly means 'inflammation of the sebaceous glands'. Lying within the dermis of the skin, closely associated with the hair follicles, the usual role of the sebaceous glands is the production of the oily substance sebum whose function is to protect and waterproof the hair and skin. In SA, the immune system of the affected individual has become targeted against the hair follicles, particularly attacking the sebaceous glands within them, which are ultimately destroyed irreversibly.

Regular grooming of a long-coated breed means you will be able to spot any signs of skin trouble at an early stage.

UROLITHS

Urolithiasis is the presence of stones or excessive amounts of crystals within the urinary tract, in the dog most commonly in the bladder. They irritate the lining of the urinary tract, resulting in pain and blood in the urine. They may predispose to a secondary bacterial infection. In some instances, they may actually partially or totally block the outflow of urine, which requires emergency treatment.

Different biochemical types of uroliths have been recognised. Surveys have found a higher than expected incidence of various types of urolithiasis in the adult Lhasa Apso with an apparent predisposition for struvite in the female (young to middle-aged), oxalate and silica in the male (middle-aged). Dietary factors are also involved.

There are two distinct patterns of disease arising from the effects of this auto-immune attack on the sebaceous glands. One group of breeds, including the Samoyed and Hungarian Vizsla, show signs of disease during the active inflammatory phase; this means that hair re-growth may occur once the sebaceous glands have been destroyed and the inflammation has resolved. The Lhasa Apso, however, falls into a second group where the signs of SA tend to develop after the active phase of inflammation as a result of the destruction of the sebaceous glands.

There is a wide spectrum of disease, with mild cases showing an initial fine dandruff with characteristically silver-coloured scaling over the head and body. More severely affected individuals develop alopecia (baldness), progressing from the head and ears initially to affect the neck and back. Recurrent secondary bacterial skin infections are common, apparent as an unpleasant musty smell, redness, scabs and itchiness (pruritus). Diagnosis is based on examining skin biopsies.

Therapy is based on shampoos to help remove scales and dead fur, and oil baths may help lubricate the skin. Supplementation of the diet with essential fatty acids is often suggested. A long course of a suitable antibiotic will be necessary when there is a secondary bacterial skin infection. Sadly, the development of resistance to the antibiotics available can lead to the need for euthanasia.

CONGENITAL HYPOTRICHOSIS

This is another skin condition seen in the Lhasa Apso. There is abnormal development of the hair follicles, which may even be absent. It becomes apparent as a permanent absence of hair from birth or developing within the first few weeks of life.

The head, ears and abdomen are commonly affected, but in more generalised cases there may only be hair on top of the head and at the extremities of the tail and legs. Diagnosis is made on the basis of a skin biopsy.

Although the general health is not affected, the skin tends to darken and become greasy, scaly and smelly. Appropriate anti-seborrhoeic shampoos may therefore be very helpful. Care must be taken to avoid sunburn, to which pale skin is susceptible, and also frostbite.

A sex-linked form of inheritance is suspected, because affected Lhasa Apsos tend to be male.

COMPLEMENTARY THERAPIES

Just as for human health, I do believe that there is a place for alternative therapies alongside and complementing orthodox treatment under the supervision of a veterinary surgeon. That is why 'complementary therapies' is a better name.

Because animals do not have a choice, there are measures in place to safeguard their wellbeing and welfare. All manipulative treatment must be under the direction of a veterinary surgeon who has examined the patient and diagnosed the condition that he or she feels needs that form of treatment. This covers physiotherapy, chiropractic, osteopathy and swimming therapy. For example, dogs with arthritis who cannot exercise as freely as they were accustomed will enjoy the sensation of controlled non-weight-bearing exercise in water, and will benefit with improved muscling and overall fitness.

All other complementary therapies such as acupuncture, homoeopathy and aromatherapy, can only be carried out by veterinary surgeons who have been trained in that particular field. Acupuncture is mainly used in dogs for pain relief, often to good effect. The needles look more alarming to the owner, but they are very fine and are well tolerated by most canine patients. Speaking personally, superficial needling is not unpleasant and does help with pain relief. Homoeopathy has had a mixed press in recent years. It is based on the concept of treating like with like. Additionally, a homoeopathic remedy is said to become more powerful the more it is diluted.

SUMMARY

As the owner of a Lhasa Apso, you are responsible for his care and health. Not only must you make decisions on his behalf, you are also responsible for

Increasingly owners are becoming aware of the benefits of complementary therapies.
© *Carol Ann Johnson*

establishing a lifestyle for him that will ensure he leads a long and happy life. Diet plays an important a part in this, as does exercise.

For the domestic dog, it is only in recent years that the need has been recognised for changing the diet to suit the dog as he grows, matures and then enters his twilight years. So-called life-stage diets try to match the nutritional needs of the dog as he progresses through life.

An adult dog food will suit the Lhasa Apso living a standard family life. There are also foods for those Lhasa Apsos tactfully termed as obese-prone, such as those who have been neutered or are less active than others, or simply like their food. Do remember, though, that ultimately you are in control of

your Lhasa Apso's diet, unless he is able to profit from scavenging!

On the other hand, prescription diets are of necessity fed under the supervision of a veterinary surgeon because each is formulated to meet the very specific needs of particular health conditions. Should a prescription diet be fed to a healthy dog, or to a dog with a different illness, there could be adverse effects.

It is important to remember that your Lhasa Apso has no choice. As his owner, you are responsible for any decision made, so it must be as informed a decision as possible. Always speak to your veterinary surgeon if you have any worries about your Lhasa Apso. He is not just a dog; from the moment you brought him home, he became a member of the family.

THE CONTRIBUTORS

THE EDITOR:
JULIETTE CUNLIFFE
(MODHISH)

Juliette Cunliffe has owned Lhasa Apsos for over 30 years, during which time she has bred and exhibited with considerable success and has had Champion and Junior Warrant winning stock. But inside the ring she is now happiest as a judge and has had the pleasure of judging Apsos, and indeed all other Tibetan breeds, in numerous different countries. Both in the UK and abroad, she is a Championship Show judge of various breeds, including of course the Lhasa Apso, which she has judged at Crufts.

It was Juliette's interest in the Lhasa Apso that first took her to the Himalaya over 20 years ago, where she has now made her home with three Apsos she took with her. Apart from being a regular columnist in the canine press, she is highly regarded throughout the world as an author, several of her books having been printed not only in English but also in German, Spanish and Russian.
See Chapter One: Getting to Know Lhasa Apsos; Chapter Two: The First Lhasa Apsos; Chapter Three: A Lhasa Apso For Your Lifestyle; Chapter Four: The New Arrival; Chapter Five: The Best of Care; Chatper Seven: The Perfect Lhasa Apso.

WENDY CAIN
(KUTANI)

Wendy has been involved with Lhasa Apsos since 1983 when she bought her first puppy from Juliette Cunliffe and Carol Ann Johnson. She was fortunate to receive good advice from the start and in her first litter produced the stunning Ch. Kutani Cincinnati who went on to win Best in Show at the Scottish Kennel Club show in 1992 and became Top Lhasa that year. Wendy followed that achievement campaigning two males who were both made Top Lhasa, one of which went Reserve Best in Show at East of England, the other winning Utility Groups. In total, Wendy has bred or shown eight UK Champions and several overseas Champions, including an International Champion, an Australian Grand Champion and an American Champion. In all, Wendy has received a grand total of 89 Challenge Certificates.
See Chapter Six: Training and Socialisation.

HELEN BELL (VALLENA)

Helen first fell in love with the Lhasa Apso whilst watching the breed on a visit to Richmond Ch Show in 1993. She bought her first show dog, who became her first champion, from Sue Ellis of the famous Nedlik affix. Since then she has made up three further champions, two of which were homebred. Helen has had the thrill of twice being awarded Best of Breed at Crufts; once in 2004 with Ch Vallena Osric who went on to take Group 4, then in 2008 with Ch Nedlik DeNato of Vallena, the judge on this occasion being Juliette Cunliffe. Since 1987 she has run her own busy grooming salon, Dashing Dogs in Luton, where she grooms all breeds, but specialises in the Lhasa Apso and Shih Tzu.
See 'Grooming' in Chapter Five: The Best of Care.

JULIA BARNES

Julia has owned and trained a number of different dog breeds, and is a puppy socialiser for Dogs for the Disabled. A former journalist, she has written many books, including several on dog training and behaviour. Julia is indebted to Wendy Cain for her knowledge about training Lhasa Apsos.
See Chapter Six: Training and Socialisation.

ALISON LOGAN MA VetMB MRCVS

Alison qualified as a veterinary surgeon from Cambridge University in 1989, having been brought up surrounded by all manner of animals and birds in the north Essex countryside. She has been in practice in her home town ever since, living with her husband, two children and Labrador Retriever Pippin.

She contributes on a regular basis to *Veterinary Times, Veterinary Nurse Times, Dogs Today, Cat World* and *Pet Patter,* the PetPlan newsletter. In 1995, Alison won the Univet Literary Award with an article on Cushing's Disease, and she won it again (as the Vetoquinol Literary Award) in 2002, writing about common conditions in the Shar-Pei.
See Chapter Eight: Happy and Healthy.

USEFUL ADDRESSES

BREED CLUBS

To obtain up-to-date contact information for the following breed clubs, please contact the Kennel Club:
- Lhasa Apso Association of Wales and South West
- Lhasa Apso Club
- Lhasa Apso Club of Scotland
- Midland Lhasa Apso Association
- North of England Lhasa Apso Club
- South East Lhasa Apso Society.

KENNEL CLUBS

American Kennel Club (AKC)
5580 Centerview Drive
Raleigh, NC 27606
Telephone: 919 233 9767
Fax: 919 233 3627
Email: info@akc.org
Web: www.akc.org

The Kennel Club (UK)
1 Clarges Street
London, W1J 8AB
Telephone: 0870 606 6750
Fax: 0207 518 1058
Web: www.the-kennel-club.org.uk

TRAINING AND BEHAVIOUR

Association of Pet Dog Trainers
PO Box 17, Kempsford, GL7 4WZ
Telephone: 01285 810811
Email: APDToffice@aol.com
Web: http://www.apdt.co.uk

Association of Pet Behaviour Counsellors
PO BOX 46, Worcester, WR8 9YS
Telephone: 01386 751151
Fax: 01386 750743
Email: info@apbc.org.uk
Web: http://www.apbc.org.uk/

ACTIVITIES

Agility Club
http://www.agilityclub.co.uk/

British Flyball Association
PO Box 990, Doncaster, DN1 9FY
Telephone: 01628 829623
Email: secretary@flyball.org.uk
Web: http://www.flyball.org.uk/

World Canine Freestyle Organisation
P.O. Box 350122, Brooklyn, NY
11235-2525, USA
Telephone: (718) 332-8336
Fax: (718) 646-2686
Email: wcfodogs@aol.com
Web: www.worldcaninefreestyle.org

HEALTH

Alternative Veterinary Medicine Centre, Chinham House, Stanford in the Vale, Oxfordshire, SN7 8NQ
Telephone: 01367 710324
Fax: 01367 718243
Web: www.alternativevet.org/

Animal Health Trust
Lanwades Park, Kentford, Newmarket, Suffolk, CB8 7UU
Telephone: 01638 751000
Web: www.aht.org.uk

British Association of Veterinary Ophthalmologists (BAVO)
Email: secretary@bravo.org.uk
Web: http://www.bravo.org.uk/

British Small Animal Veterinary Association
Woodrow House, 1 Telford Way,
Waterwells Business Park, Quedgeley,
Gloucestershire, GL2 2AB
Telephone: 01452 726700
Fax: 01452 726701
Email: customerservices@bsava.com
Web: http://www.bsava.com/

British Veterinary Hospitals Association
Station Bungalow, Main Rd,
Stocksfield, Northumberland,
NE43 7HJ
Telephone: 07966 901619
Fax: 07813 915954
Email: office@bvha.org.uk
Web: http://www.bvha.org.uk/

Royal College of Veterinary Surgeons
Belgravia House, 62-64 Horseferry Road, London, SW1P 2AF
Telephone: 0207 222 2001
Fax: 0207 222 2004
Email: admin@rcvs.org.uk
Web: www.rcvs.org.uk

ASSISTANCE DOGS

Canine Partners
Mill Lane, Heyshott, Midhurst,
West Sussex, GU29 0ED
Telephone: 08456 580480
Fax: 08456 580481
Web: www.caninepartners.co.uk

Dogs for the Disabled
The Frances Hay Centre, Blacklocks Hill,
Banbury, Oxon, OX17 2BS
Telephone: 01295 252600
Web: www.dogsforthedisabled.org

Guide Dogs for the Blind Association
Burghfield Common, Reading,
RG7 3YG
Telephone: 01189 835555
Fax: 01189 835433
Web: www.guidedogs.org.uk/

Hearing Dogs for Deaf People
The Grange, Wycombe Road,
Saunderton, Princes Risborough,
Bucks, HP27 9NS
Telephone: 01844 348100
Fax: 01844 348101
Web: www.hearingdogs.org.uk

Pets as Therapy
3a Grange Farm Cottages, Wycombe
Road, Saunderton, Princes Risborough,
Bucks, HP27 9NS
Telephone: 01845 345445
Fax: 01845 550236
Web: http://www.petsastherapy.org/

Support Dogs
21 Jessops Riverside, Brightside Lane,
Sheffield, S9 2RX
Tel: 01142 617800
Fax: 01142 617555
Email: supportdogs@btconnect.com
Web: www.support-dogs.org.uk

puppy
sponsor

Dogs for the
Disabled

Help us turn paws into helping hands

Sponsor a **Dogs for the Disabled** puppy for just £5.00 per
month and you could help change someone's life.

Dogs for the
Disabled
Registered charity number: 1092960

www.dogsforthedisabled.org   Telephone: 01295 252600